About the Author

CL (Clare) Rolfe lives in the Southern Highlands NSW, Australia. Inspired by her love for travelling, art, reading and the admiration for people who had overcome significant hardships she encountered during her time working in healthcare, she began to focus on her writing rather than just daydreaming about the stories in her mind. Ten Letters is her first published work and along with philosophizing, she also dabbles in poetry and short stories.

To connect with CL Rolfe find her on Facebook or twitter @rolfe_cl or clrolfe.wordpress.com

Copyright CL Rolfe 2016

First Published in Australia by CL Rolfe in 2016

CL Rolfe is the sole author of this book

This book is a work of fiction and except in the case of historical references and persons, then any resemblance to actual persons, living or dead, is purely coincidental

This book remains the copyrighted property of the author, and may not be redistributed to others for commercial or non-commercial purposes. If you enjoyed this book, please encourage your friends to obtain their own copy from their favourite authorized retailer. Thank you for your support.

Printed and distributed by Ingramspark

Cover design CL Rolfe

Ten Letters to Delacroix's Tomb

by CL Rolfe © 2016

'I live in company with a body, a silent companion, exacting and eternal. He it is who notes that individuality which is the seal of the weakness of our race. My soul has wings, but the brutal jailer is strict.'

Eugene Delacroix (1798-1863)

1 Letter Last

In your eyes I see a thousand years have passed and in their sight I see a thousand years to come. In your deep pools of antiquity my small life found its purpose and the solace of understanding where my feet should stand in the world.

Were you a god that placed your eyes upon me at the sound of my lost footsteps and took pity on the imprisoned soul? Or were you a nomadic heart lost like me? Could a god ever lose its way such as those of us who tread beneath its gaze, battered and dismayed at what must be borne along the road?

I remember the vision of eternity never faded from your sight even when the light of day died and there was only shadow and hopeless pain.

I am called now to staunch this bleeding wound and see the end days at your side. The first step begins as the sun wanes. Expect me upon the first indigo sky and rise of the black dawn.

I am coming dear heart.

'Jenna, come help!'

Jenna put the quill down and rolled the last piece of parchment and tied it with a red ribbon. The bow seemed out of place on the battered piece of compressed tree but it was a formal touch which would signal the importance of the note. The ribbon was tattered with stained edges. She remembered the first time she had found the reel of bright material. How her heart had jumped at the prettiness of it. Her tilling the soil had disturbed its rest. When she opened the box, the dust of ancient paper flew into the air. Inside laid the treasure of the red ribbon; perfectly coiled. There had been just enough to wrap this last message.

The bow became squashed as she pushed the note into the reed tube to protect it along the journey. The kestrel fluttered and pecked as she tied the parcel to its leg.

Taking it outside as she released it into the cerise sky a feather drifted down. The bird soared in the direction she expected but different to the one she would take. She felt sad as she watched it disappear. She had found it as a chick and raised it. Safe journey little one, she whispered. Picking up a small pouch made from leather she rolled her quill into it and tucked it inside her tunic along with the feather.

'Here bitch' yelled Adrik 'Take this.'

Jenna looked at the ruddy pock marked skin and jaundiced eyes. Her heart no longer swelled with anger and hatred like it once had but now seemed detached at the man called her master. She snatched the rope before it smacked her in the face. Taking it she tied it to the boat that bumped against the edge of the sludgy river bank.

Mary came over with three sacks of grain. She whispered under her breath aware of Adrik's agitation.

'It is the last of the stores but we at least have something to barter with.'

Jenna didn't say anything as she went to load more of the cargo. She looked at Mary as she walked past, her heart sparking instantly with annoyance. She saw the scars on the woman's neck; still raw where the brand had landed when Adrik found grit in the stew two nights ago. Jenna actually thought Mary had moved forward to take the punishment. She looked away and went to where their shawls and jackets lay before the loathing made her say something.

'Soon, soon, be patient slave.' The words came back to her. They had been spoken a time long ago now to Jenna's memory. The toothless smile of the old Chinese man came back with the words.

Slave back then had had no meaning and it still didn't to Jenna. Mary: yes Mary was. She had become the bonded and chained, but not herself.

The night descended quickly as the three sat around the remains of a feeble fire. The hut looked bare, even barer than usual. Everything had been burned or packed in the boat. Jenna's cheek still throbbed from a slap Adrik had given her earlier when she had tripped on a log and spilt some of the fresh water.

'It won't matter Adrik. They will draw the numbers again. My Grandmother spoke of that...' the next thing she remembered was reeling on the ground, her ears ringing and nose bleeding from the vicious strike. As she had risen for just a second their eyes met and she thought she saw the fear that clung to him and the understanding why her defiance had not ended in death many times over. She had stared him down as his hunched form lumbered its way to the boat with the clay urn. She knew more than him. That was Adrik's weakness, all power and control had been given to men like him and yet he still did not wield it to any advantage; simply because he did not know how. He sat here like a rat on a sinking ship clinging to an ignorant hope the dogmatic forces that had made him, would rescue him again. He was as bonded as much as the rest of us. He hadn't spoken to her since that moment and the boat had been packed in silence the rest of the day.

Jenna went into her room to lie down. In the darkened hut she heard the sounds of Mary's continued abuse. It still made her stomach lurch. She had tried to protect Mary in the beginning but when the simple woman had taken hold of her arm to stop her hitting Adrik on that first night so long ago, Jenna had realized it would be futile to try and defend her at risk to herself.

'You should be grateful I am the one to bear this Jenna and not you.' Mary's words had stung forcing deep hatred to well in Jenna's heart at that moment. How dare you when you are so degraded and willing to take the humiliation he spews onto you? She had stormed off barely able to contain her rage. Deep down though she knew Mary was right. Jenna had conquered no one, least of all Adrik. Even without education and knowledge, Mary served her own purpose as well. One that offered more protection to Jenna then she could give back to Mary. So who was the slave after all? Mary's simple wisdom spoke more of the world and what it had always been than anything she remembered her grandmother reading to her. It was this truth that hurt the most. An image of a god carrying the world on its shoulders had come to mind. Atlas he had been called. How could Mary be her Atlas and yet it was the truth. That's why the slaves were bred in the first place; for one purpose alone to carry the heavy loads for the Bondmasters.

Jenna called to mind her grandmother's face to help her fall asleep. The old woman's eyes were dark velvety brown and so large amongst the folds of skin that hung around them, you could feel yourself become lost in their warmth. When those eyes gazed at you they looked into your very being. The old woman would sit and talk of times gone by when there was plenty for all and the world was less worried with its survival.

'Live civilly with kindness in your hearts, as arrogance will serve no purpose. Be not a slave or a master but a prophet for those who remain. Teach what you know, where you can, so others may have the chance to learn who they are and where their feet stand in the world. You children don't know how lucky you are to hear one of your kin speak like this. To speak of times when the world was green and the sky was blue; when reading the great thoughts and ideas of the age of antiquity and the echoes of the heart mattered as much as feeding the body's needs. A time when humans loved and fought over their own petty desires as they thought them more important than trying to save a dying sun.'

'What do they fight for now Grandmother?' Jack had asked.

'They don't fight Jack, they wait for death. All passion and selfish desire has been killed off so that now everyone must walk the path chosen with no choice. Along with it has been lost our spirit that makes us who we are. A tiger only knows how to be a tiger but we can know how to be ourselves and the tiger.'

The lessons had been taught rigorously without compromise to the three of them; Kat, Jack and herself. The stories of wars, of gods who avenged and struck down men and ones who saved and others that gave wise words. It was unfathomable to Jenna's mind then as a child, and even now as an old woman that people had had the time to think of such things. Their grandmother had made them learn to read and study thick unwieldy tablets of florid language. Her mind had reeled at all the words written throughout the history of the world and how irrelevant it seemed now. There were so many stories of love for each other. At the time Jenna had not understood the passion that could consume a heart. Not until she had been wrenched away from her home and forced into her pre-ordained destiny.

Jenna rolled over and placed a wheat sack on her ear to block out the sounds coming from Mary. She let her mind drift to when she was a child. She had worn jeans and a jumper and hat. Her hair was bleached white not like the dirty mat it was now. Grandmother was sitting on the veranda scrubbing pumpkins to preserve them. It was easy preserving, there was so much salt in the earth that it made sense to preserve it. 'Salt of the earth.' Where had that saying come from? It was an expression she had heard her grandmother say so many times. She said it meant that the salt enriched the earth by its presence. All Jenna knew now was how it killed the earth. It erupted in great patches from the soil as the sun drew it out.

'Children you won't have to do it all alone. There will be others but just remember, now it's thin on the ground.'

She had been skipping when she heard Grandmother say this to Kat and Jack as they sat helping her. They both nodded.

'But Grandmother, it all seems silly to be doing anything. After all it will all end and it won't make a difference.' said Kat.

'It does matter Katlin, because they said even when I was a little girl like Jenna, that it would end but now there have been three generations since those words. False prophets! It matters. Each moment requires living. It still needs to be done well: even if it means scrubbing these orange skinned rocks. If we don't do it we die and therefore it matters because it will make a difference to us living or dying. Make each step along the way purposeful and strong.'

'Grandmother I was reading a book about Paris. I will go there one day. The book spoke of an artist called Rodin who made a statue about thinking. I would like to see what thinking looks like.'

'Don't be stupid Jen! No one goes anywhere any more. It's not allowed and besides it probably doesn't exist. Also books don't speak.' Kat had retorted.

Jenna remembered the haughty manner of her sister as vividly as her grandmother's eyes. She drifted into sleep with a thin smile on her face.

Dawn came slowly and was only noticed by the grey stillness that came with it. Getting up Jenna saw Adrik already at the boat. Her mind felt clearer this morning. She would leave once they had neared the coastal settlement to the south. There would be traders she could bribe.

Mary gestured to her 'Come eat Jen. It isn't much but the chaff at the bottom at least made porridge.'

She took the bowl that Mary thrust before her.

'It's our last meal here.'

Jenna sat on the window sill. Last meal the words evoked an image of something called the last supper. What did that mean? Grandmother had stitched a tapestry. She had called it the Last Supper. The cloth had been laid on the table. The faces had faded but the vibrant red and blue of the robes had taken the longest time to dull.

'Yes it is the last meal Mary. You should use this time to look elsewhere for a master. We can choose now not to be bonded together.'

'Adrik is not the worst there is Jen. After all he lets you stay here when you are not needed.'

Jenna smiled to herself at the asinine comment. Jenna had been told that same thing on countless other occasions by Kat as well as former masters. Even when she first went to Paris, she had been told she was not wanted.

'When things worsen again Jen, they will want the people like me, willing to follow.'

'Maybe Mary.'

Jenna had never told Adrik or Mary of what they walked to. She understood more than ever now the value of the lessons Grandmother had taught.

'Knowledge gives you the power to know where to tread next and the sense to know when to take those steps and when to pause and just watch the sunset.' chimed her grandmother's voice. Jenna finished the porridge knowing that the time was now to begin her journey home.

'Get goin' yelled their master.

Jenna looked at the bruises on Mary's face and arms. Her heart thudded as she attempted one last time to convince Mary to seek her freedom.

'It's interesting Mary that Adrik never wanted a male slave. After all, what two women can do, one man can do more. You choose not to see it. You choose not to see what a coward he really is. You choose to be the slave because we all have to be something Mary.'

'I dunno what you're talking about. My slaver father used to thrash me more than Adrik ever has. I remember his own cuts and lashes bleeding from his days working in the mines as he beat me and my guardian mother. You don't appreciate what you have here. Why are you always causing trouble Jenna?'

Jenna stopped herself from saying anything more. Once again the simple honesty about the world from this slave's mouth had made her feel foolish and cut deeply with its hopelessness. She let Mary go ahead. Waiting until Mary's and Adrik's attention was elsewhere she pulled the shaved paddle she had hidden out from under a pile of hessian sacks and stashed it inside her tunic. It sat near the pouch. Its awkward hardness hurt against her breast unlike the other treasure.

Getting into the boat she helped push it from the bank through the sludge and reeds. Jenna looked back at the makeshift hut and the small patches of farming around it as they paddled further into the river. She had been bonded to this place almost eighteen years. Mary was wrong about why Adrik had kept her. Jenna knew how to farm and he didn't.

'I have survived by my knowledge not by the blood of your abuse. Be careful Mary, he knows the truth of it.' she thought to herself.

The river crept amongst the silent mangroves. It was still cool and the streaks of the sunrise danced weakly on the small currents the skiff made. Jenna looked at Mary and Adrik from behind. Both were slouched and silent, worn down just like the world around them.

'It will be as if I never met either of you, so distant is my heart and mind from you both. What were each of you before we came to be here? You won't even be a memory that occasionally surfaces to remind me of where I have been and who I am. You are the detritus that floats on the surface of the river and out into the great heaving oceans; only to be swallowed and forgotten. Leave now Mary! When he realises there is no escape then he will be more lethal than anything you have ever known.

'Steer straight!' yelled Adrik as they neared the small waterfall. The boat tipped. Mary almost fell out. Adrik scowled.

'Hold her steady, ya useless whore!'

Jenna held the oar tightly trying to stop the skiff capsizing. The blisters on her calloused hands broke as the tenacious grip of the water on the paddle tore her flesh. The resistance of the current made the muscles in her arms burn but she did not give in and managed to guide them over the frothing turbulence. They rowed until the river turned to the south. The bend was so sharp that Jenna lost sight of the curving grey water as the thick greenery of the mangrove swamps blocked her view. As they emerged she could see a settlement of fishermen in the distance. Smoke rose from the ground and drifted delicately over the water. Its fine tendrils looked like fingers stroking the supple current of the river. A memory of hands tenderly stroking her back made her shiver. She sat up and looked at the village as it grew nearer. Jenna had only been here once in her time with Adrik. The huts were a replica of their own, except instead of wheat and pumpkins in piles there were carp strung from the rafters of the tiny verandahs. A young girl stared as she washed her clothes in the water. She did not smile but looked through them like they didn't exist.

She looks like Kat, Jenna thought.

'How long to the coast?' asked Mary.

'Another day Mary. It lies at least 30 miles from here.' replied Jenna

'How do you know? Is that true Adrik?' Mary asked.

Adrik didn't say anything.

Jenna didn't bother answering. He doesn't know either, she thought. He has never been to the south coast. That's why he brought me. He could have left me. I could have stayed at the farm until the end times but he needed me to guide him to where he thinks he will be safe. It will serve us both.

Jenna let herself ease into the flow of the river. The current had begun to pick up pace and made the paddling easier. In her mind lay images of ruptured stone roads and decaying buildings. The man made ruins seemed beautiful in their demise as the white marble trimmed with rusted iron lacework slowly disintegrated into the earth that it had come from. She saw herself walking to a blue doorway and knocking. It opened.

Suddenly a loud bang broke Jenna's daydreaming. Over to her right in the distance she saw smoke rising out of the ground. Another wave of noise hit them.

'Get down! It's the militia!' hissed Adrik.

'Get over to the shore to hide under there!' He pointed to a massive tree overhanging the opposite bank. They paddled frantically, shoving the skiff's bow under the thick branches.

The vibrations of another loud explosion rippled across the sky and water, making the boat rock.

'Godammit, we will have to go to the north. Fucking fools. What's the point?'

'What are they?'

Adrik didn't answer Mary's question.

Jenna saw Adrik's panic stricken eyes watching between the branches to see if the Purgers were coming towards them.

'They are part of the Bondmasters Mary. They are purging the towns and villages. They are fools Adrik. It is a waste of time now.'

'Shut up! They could be in the swamps!' Adrik spat at Jenna knowing how dangerous the militia of Purgers could be. It had been the Bondmasters that had formed them long ago when the first of the long winters began; created to stop disease and keep food plentiful for the few who would survive the dark seasons.

Silence stayed with them for a long time. When the sky began to turn pink and dusk was on its way Adrik pushed the skiff out into the water cautiously. The wind had been blowing south so the smell of the destruction did not greet them. They all scanned the far side of the river alert to any sign the Purgers may still be close.

They rowed out far enough to avoid being entangled in the branches. Jenna could just see in the dim twilight the fork in the river. One direction would lead south and the other north.

'Take the north.'

Jenna's heart raced at Adrik's barely audible command. It would take them towards the great northern sea. Jenna had sailed it once and knew its treachery. There would be no trader ships to stow away upon.

'If the purge has already been south then it would be safer to go south.' probed Jenna.

No answer came back telling her, that they would not be going that way.

Doreng- 12, the place they were heading to could only be reached from the north by crossing the great plateau of Myanmar rather than along the coastal routes. When we reach the delta of the river I could make my way back to the southern route. No the mud flats extended for miles. Adrik would be able to catch her.

'Be patient slave. There will be a chance to run.' She muttered trying to still the rising panic in her chest.

Darkness fell heavily. The moth eaten moon was on the wane and the stars were blocked from the falling embers of the sun. The black dawn approaches Jenna thought as her eyes adjusted to the night. Suddenly a memory of her grandmother reading a tablet to her came back.

'As fewer solar flares explode from the surface of the sun they will become more intense. And as they reach the magnetic field of the earth they will disintegrate into black particulates. This matter will build with time and become so thick that the stars and moon will fade from our view and even the yellow rays of the sun will not rise on the dawn but rather appear black with streaks of deep indigo like a night sky that never ends.'

'Those words are dense and heavy on your tongue when you read them Grandmother.'

'Yes they are but they are true. '

'When will the black dawn happen?'

'No one knows. A time when we could educate ourselves about this and predict its coming ended before we figured it out. We live too much from day to day now and when the long winters starve us there are too few left to have time to ponder such problems. Even the Bondmasters cannot survive as too many of the slaves die. So they have to work also and cannot learn or dwell on things that are not necessary. But all you will need to know dear is when the moon and stars finally disappear then it will be the birth of the winter that will last forever and the rise of the never ending black dawns.'

'Can we read something else?'

'I have frightened you.'

'Hmm a little. It actually sounds like it would be beautiful to see a black dawn.'

'Yes I thought the same thing the first time my grandmother read this to me as well.'

'Gosh it must be old!' Jenna had giggled.

She remembered snuggling into her grandmother's fleshy arms and bosom and thinking that the old woman radiated more warmth and love than the sun ever did. The day her grandmother died then that would be her black dawn. That was so long ago but the memory made it seem like yesterday. I wish I had more time with you. I never wanted to let you go. Tears began to roll down Jenna's cheeks at the memory of her lost happiness. She was glad that the darkness hid her sorrow from Adrik and Mary. She willed the images back to their safe place in her heart to stop more tears being spilled. The time for sadness was over now. Grief was a luxury she couldn't afford.

As the red haze of the sunrise began to reflect in the water the sound of the skiff dragging on the river bed roused them all.

'Haul er up' called Adrik.

Mary and Jenna jumped out and sank knee deep into the silt. The river was tepid and its current helped them pull the boat to the bank. Soon they had moved it onto dry ground.

'Cover it up' hissed Adrik.

Jenna nearly blurted out why but decided not to. She needed Adrik to be calm and pliable. There was no grog here where she could get him to sleep and even if there was some to buy she would need to save the barter coins for the journey.

The day grew brighter as they climbed from the delta of the river into the foothills above. Jenna saw her path home disappearing with every step as they walked north towards the plateau villages.

The sack of wheat sat comfortably on her back and her hidden treasures remained safe. Tonight, she thought. I will walk until it is dark and then I will flee. He can follow me too easily in the day.

'Jenna are you ok? You keep looking over your shoulder.' called Mary.

'Yes Mary, just making sure none of them are following us.'

'Uh ok.' Mary turned and trotted to catch Adrik who was striding ahead of them.

Soon the canopy of the forest disappeared unveiling the wide treeless plains of the plateau of Myanmar. It stretched a thousand miles to the north. She watched the lumbering walk of Adrik and Mary's defeated slouch ahead of her as she tried to think of a way to escape before she was too far from the coast. He would have to put the urns of water down to chase her. They are too awkward to run with. He would not like to leave the precious stuff for too long.

The sun rose higher and Jenna began to feel the heat. Her mouth was dry and her lips cracked.

'Adrik we need to rest a little.'

'Keep goin'! I don't want to waste any more time.'

Deciding she needed to slow the pace of their hiking she loosened the strap on the sack of grain and then tripped over. Half the grain spilled out onto the grass. She lay still until suddenly she felt the roughness of Adrik's hand on her neck as he hoisted her up.

'Get up you fucking bitch before I beat you!'

'I need to rest a little Adrik. Mary aren't you tired?'

'I am. It is hotter up here.' Jenna smiled at seeing Mary drink from one of the urns and sit herself down without permission.

Adrik scowled at the pair of them. Jenna watched him puff and wheeze as he stooped to gather the grain into the sack. His brow was sweaty and spittle lay on his lips.

'I will do that. It was my fault.' He looked at her and flung the rope that tied the bag at her and strode off. He went over to a rock and sat on it and took a swig out of one of the urns as well.

Jenna tried to guess the time by looking up at the pale sun. It was after midday so it would be dusk in a few hours.

'Enuff. Get up!'

Adrik collected the water and started walking. Mary sprang up and took her sacks. As Jenna began to walk she dragged her left leg.

'What the fuck is wrong now?'

'I've hurt my foot.'

'Keep up or I will flog you.' He snarled.

She didn't answer. Soon her back ached and calves burned from the feigned limping but she could feel the coolness of dusk nearing. Not long now and I will be free. Adrik and Mary were at least half a mile ahead of her.

She watched his back sway and his arms. She could feel the weight of the shaved down paddle. She sensed the closeness of the pouch to her heart and was comforted knowing it was still safe and unknown to the world.

She watched the sun dip below the mountains of Old Myanmar in the distance. As the last rays clung to the highest peaks the light suddenly changed to purple, signaling the dusk. She fell panting.

'I can't go any further today Adrik.' He turned and saw her lying in the grass. She waited. Mary followed behind him obediently.

'You have slowed us down enough. GET UP.' She saw his hand swing ready to slap her. Grabbing the paddle she shot it up and felt it connect with his throat. His hand came down but with hardly any force. She thrust it again sinking it into his gut, winding him. Taking advantage she viciously struck his knee. He stumbled as his leg gave way from under him. Mary screamed and went to stop her. Jenna swung at her, knocking her out. Adrik got up re-gathering himself as he uncoiled his whip. But Jenna rushed him and pushed him over. She was surprised how little resistance met her. Straddling him and with all her force she brought the paddle down. He went limp as the crunch of his nose breaking penetrated the stillness of the night. She hesitated above him wanting to inflict the lethal strike but couldn't. In her heart she couldn't be like him. Instead she took his whip and turning him over tied his hands and feet. Jenna never forgot how he had tenaciously tracked her down the last time she had tried to escape. She had barely survived the beating. She tied Mary with some of the rope from the sacks of grain as well.

She stood and noticed that the other two sacks of wheat had fallen over and one of the urns had smashed. The grain had spilt everywhere and the water lost into the soil. The waste of it almost made her sob. She retied the sack she was carrying and left the rest. She wasn't cruel. There would be enough for Adrik and Mary. Whatever hope lay in the hearts of these two they would need that food; there would be no more coming.

Hoisting the wheat up onto her shoulder she ran back towards the coast. Vaguely she heard groans. Jenna ran blindly in the utter blankness of the night guided by the sounds of the waves crashing on the shore. The only thing that was visible was the face of Gabriel before her.

'It is not our time to end.' His voice echoed in her heart.

'I am coming dear heart.' She answered into the darkness.

2 Letter Nine

I was bonded permanently today. He is a cruel master. He hit me then lashed me. The blood clots in my hair as I lie in a shack on the coast of old Siam.

He saw me in the trader's stalls signing my name in blood and knows I have knowledge. I heard him say I would be trouble so I said my back was strong and I know the seasons of the lands from my time with the reeders. I looked him in the eye and he knows I will not bend to one such as him. It will be difficult for us all.

His land lies to the north of the coast at the beginning of a river. The soil is black and fertile, and the long winters from old China ensure there is plenty of fresh water to nourish the soil and streams.

I chose this master for I can grow strong on the food I will grow in his land. While my heart and mind were fed by the old man's words in China, the flesh and bones have withered from the harshness of life amongst the stony mountains. Here I can wash the blood that oozes from my broken body so it may heal and remain sturdy so that when the black dawn rises it will be ready to begin the journey home.

This is my last trial, my heavy stone that I push up the hill, as my grandmother used to say. This time will be the darkness before the light. This is the beginning of the end of the story of the exiled slave. The lost sparrow seeks its home and nothing will stop its flight.

I dip my quill in the blood from my torn flesh to write this letter not knowing if it will reach you.

My first tentative steps back to the road that leads to your door have been taken.

I am coming dear heart

Jenna's heart thudded as she walked the gravel road into the village. The bleakness of the day was not lifted by the vista of the coastline opening before her, rather it only added to her feeling of unease. In the distance she saw a large majestic home, well maintained and out of place amongst the primitive huts of the village that lay nestled beneath. Her legs and back ached constantly now. She had been walking for thirty days since leaving Adrik and Mary.

'Heya traveler!' called the voice close behind her. It made Jenna jump at the sudden noise.

She turned and saw a young man walking with a herd of emaciated goats. It had been so long since she had spoken to someone she had no idea what to say. Blood rushed in her ears as the panic at meeting someone began to rise.

'I am Yan. Where have you come from?'

'I have, um I am from…' Jenna almost burst into tears as she tried desperately to say something.

Finally she took a deep breath as she watched Yan patiently wait for her answer.

'I have been released from my Bondmaster and I am making my way back to where I came from.'

'And where is that?'

No I don't want to tell you because you will not believe and you are so young you will not know of it. It is my story not yours.

'It is far from here Yan; unknown to these lands.'

'Yes you look different to us. Come ah…' he looked quizzically at Jenna as she had not told him her name.

'Oh Jenna. My name is Jenna.'

Yan smiled and nodded. 'Come Jenna.'

'I come only to replenish supplies Yan.'

Yan waved his arm indicating she should follow him.

The goats walked around her and bleated as they passed. She smiled at their indifference and obedience to their shepherd. She took a deep breath trying to still her heart and followed Yan into the village.

He strode to a hut that had a yard fenced off at its side. He pushed the goats into the makeshift pen. Jenna hesitated not sure of what to do.

'Please come inside.'

'I really only want to buy some more grain, if there is any to be bought?'

'There is nothing now. The store masters will have put everything away. You might as well rest this evening.'

Jenna nodded reluctantly. She went into the small dwelling. Inside was just as gloomy as outside.

A young woman stood up from a fire in the corner upon which sat a pot with bubbling liquid. The smoke from the fire mixed with the steam rising from the pot and floated out a window just above the hearth.

'Ru Li, this is Jenna.'

She nodded towards the small woman as she bowed. Ru Li looked at Jenna for a moment but did not say anything. Jenna noticed the bowed legs and stooped back from the malnourished childhood.

'Please sit.' Yan removed his cloak and Ru Li ladled some soup into two bowls.

She handed Yan and Jenna one each. Ru Li then took another ladle and scooped some out of the pot and drank it.

'I should not be eating your food like this.'

'There is enough. Eat.' Spoke Yan, 'The master does not abide the village to be unwelcoming to strangers.'

'What is the name of the village?' asked Jenna

'Kingston Cove.'

Jenna stopped just as she was to eat the first mouthful of soup when she heard the name. It was the same name as the place where she had grown up.

'I am in the lands of Singapore aren't I?' she asked

'Oh yes but the first Bondmaster renamed this placed when he settled here.'

'It is an unusual name. I have not heard of it before.'

Yan and Ru Li did not answer, unaware of Jenna's lie.

'Have the Purgers been through your lands?'

'No the master will not allow them.'

'How is that possible? The Purgers are no….' Jenna stopped before she said anything more. It would be strange for a bonded to have knowledge about the Purgers.

'We do not know. The master's father set it down when he first settled here.'

Jenna nodded. The Bondmaster's leashes had broken long ago and now their pets had become a militia ruled only by their genetic perfection. More perfect in their strength and tenacity then what the earth had intended for her creatures. They were relentless in their duty.

'Where have you come from?'

'I came from Siam, above the river.'

'And now you travel to your home.'

'Where is that?' asked Ru Li.

'It…is…called..' Jenna had never told anyone where her heart lay. Not even the old man in China. She didn't want anyone to know in case they took it away from her. It had been with her so long, as her kernel of joy to break the poverty of her life. It was unspoken like all things the soul wishes for; which if uttered on the lips seemed to only make them disappear along with the hope that lies with them.

'I am going to a settler town called Van Diemen's isle. It is on the northern tip of old Oceania.' Jenna replied.

Ru Li took the empty stone bowls and went out to a small well to wash them. Yan straightened a quilt of reed clothe and lay down.

Darkness came but it was not cold as the humidity trapped by the mountains clung to the village. Jenna lay outside with her swag under her and shawl for a blanket. She felt the leather pouch that nestled close to her thudding heart. It helped calm her. It was still safe; the world had not penetrated that deeply. She was grateful for the kindness from the shepherd and his wife. She drifted between memory and sleep. She was walking towards the old door. It was daubed with the faintest of blue. It was very old. Its wrinkled exterior matched the face of the old man of China. Its broken edges blended with the crumbling stone path she walked on. She knocked on the door and waited. It didn't move. It remained still. For some reason she could see every detail of the wood knots, the grains imprinted there long before she had lived. It breathed her in and expelled her as if to say what a minute detail you are compared to me. It opened as if it had suddenly taken pity on her.

'It is daylight again.'

Jenna stirred at the sound of Yan's voice. Her head was heavy and body aching unbelievably.

'I slept too well.' She tried to get up but couldn't. Yan put his hand out to help her stand. She took it and almost screamed as her body resisted the movement.

Panting she leant against the post of the goat's pen.

'Take some water and soup.' Jenna nodded and stumbled into the hut. Ru Li offered her to sit.

'I don't think I will be able to stand up again if I do.'

She leant against the small window sill as she ate her breakfast.

'Is there somewhere I can buy some grain today?'

'Yes Kim will have some. There is not much to buy. The harvests grow poorer every season.'

'I will only need enough to make it to Singapore Bay.'

'Why don't you stay another night? You look tired.' said Ru Li

'I am tired but I have been delayed long enough. I fear time grows short as it is.'

'How will you get to the southern lands?'

'I worked with a trader there once on the reeder boats. I will seek passage with one of them.'

Jenna drank her soup quickly. She didn't want any more questions about her journey. She stood and threw her swag across her back and made her way outside.

'I will walk with you Jenna.' Her heart sunk a little but there was no point in saying no to Yan. Perhaps it was just friendly interest.

'Ok.'

They walked down toward the coastline. The huts were built along the narrow strip of land between the ocean and the mountains. A road hewn many generations ago wound between the dwellings on either side. The roar of the waves battering the cliffs broke the grey silence of the village. Dominating the face of the mountain was the large mansion of the Bondmaster. It reminded Jenna of a great sentinel watching the ocean. It stood as if in warning to the sea, this part of the world is not your dominion.

Jenna saw a small humpy with sacks sitting around its door.

'Is this the grain Yan?'

'Yes its Kim's place. He will sell you some.'

The humpy abutted the water's edge in a protected inlet. Behind it, bobbing in the water was a boat. It was large enough to carry three people and supplies.

'Heya Kim.' called Yan.

A wizened old man came out. Jenna looked at the rivulets of age on his face and looked into his bright intelligent eyes. He suddenly broke into a toothless smile and bowed to them both.

'Heya Yan. You surprised me I thought it was the master.' spoke Kim.

'Kim this is Jenna. She wants to barter some grain.'

'I have only this left now.' Yan gestured to the half dozen sacks at his doorway

'One will be enough. The boat over there, is it seaworthy?'

'It will need some fixing.'

'I have some new seeds for planting I can give you. They are pumpkin and rye. They will grow in the rocky soils here and the stock will produce bountiful harvests.'

Kim raised his eyebrows at the gesture.

'New seeds to plant a crop are precious and worth more than coins.'

Jenna removed a small bag latched to her waist sash.

'It will be enough for you and Yan and most of the village with time. I had more but my journey here has been a long one.'

She swallowed knowing that the seeds would have one maybe two harvest left but then again so would the villagers. It was all she had to offer.

'Yan come inside.'

Jenna looked at Yan wondering if there was a problem

'It is alright Jenna; normally the men do the barter not the women. It is our way.'

Jenna nodded slightly relieved.

The shepherd followed Kim inside the humpy.

Jenna went over to the boat to inspect it. The hull had two patches that needed tar and the mast was not repairable. A new one would be needed. I can row down to Old Border town and find some new timber there she thought. Cloth would be easy or if she needed her shawl and blanket could be re-sown. Her eyes darted around taking in all the detail and the possibilities of what the boat could offer her.

Suddenly there was a sound of crunching gravel behind her. She hid behind the humpy. Inside she heard Kim and Yan quietly talking. She peered around the edge of the mud wall and saw a man being pulled by two other men in a cart. He was like her, fair skinned with a thick mat of dirty grey blonde hair. He had a hat on and blue cravat that radiated its brightness like a patch of sky in the grey pall of the morning. It must be the Bondmaster she thought to herself. Her heart began to pound. Adrik's face came to mind. She watched the cart as it meandered its way to a fork in the road. It took the path that lead toward the mansion.

Finally Kim and Yan emerged with broad smiles.

'It is a deal but the boat will need to be repaired. It is part of our bond agreement with the master that we are honourable in our barters. Yan and I will fix the mast and hull.' spoke Kim

'So you will need to stay another night at least.' Yan beamed at her.

She capitulated knowing that she could not repair the boat herself. It would be better to stay. It would save her time if the boat was fully fixed now. She would only need to find food in Old Singapore Bay.

She looked at the willing pair and felt a pang of sorrow at their generosity. Would they believe me that I had not been honourable with them? Would they believe me if I told them that the seeds will give you one or two fine feasts and then all will wither? It is beyond all of us now. I am glad I can give you this bit of pleasure and that we both have these kindnesses to offer each other.

'Thank you that is very generous Kim and Yan. One more night it is then.'

'Go back to Ru Li. She will be milking the goats and may need help.'

Yan dismissed her as he handed her the sacks of grain. She bowed at them as he and Kim walked to the boat to haul it up onto the shore.

She pulled her shawl up and over her head to hide herself as much as possible. She looked up at the large house again. The cart had gone and the windows remained fixed on the ocean and some lost horizon. Hopefully it would only be one more night and she would be drifting in the safety of the ocean; far away from Masters and Purgers.

She found Ru Li wrestling with a goat as she tried to tie it to a post. Jenna caught the beast by its head to settle it down. Ru Li hastily looped the rope around the post and pulled it tight.

'Do you know how to milk? It will be quicker with the two of us.'

'Yes. I can milk her.'

Soon she and Ru Li were in a rhythm together. Jenna lost herself to the enjoyment of the task. She had missed the routine of waking to do chores since she had left Adrik and Mary. Lost in her thoughts the time passed quickly. She realised as she took another goat it was the last one. Her back and hands ached in satisfaction that she had earned her keep.

Ru Li went inside and Jenna followed. They took some soup together in the pallor of the remaining daylight. As it faded into the night Yan stepped into the hut.

'It goes well Jenna. We have fixed the boat but the mast will need another day maybe two for the tar to set.'

Jenna's heart sunk at the news.

'You need the rest Jenna.' Spoke Ru Li

'One more day Yan. That is all.'

Jenna slept fitfully that night as her mind filled with images of being caged. Her boat lay struggling in the waves unable to sail as the rope that lashed it to its moorings held fast and would not let go. She sobbed, not now. Let me be free!

Waking suddenly she heard footsteps. She looked and saw the back of Yan disappearing down the hill.

Jenna stood feeling exhausted and depressed. The day was darker than usual as a storm loomed over the ocean. Ru Li came out of the hut wrapping a scarf around her head; near the doorway stood two black urns. They were perfectly sculpted with two handles for carrying placed symmetrically on either side.

'I have to take some of the goat milk to the master. Can you help me carry them?'

Jenna knew she couldn't really say no but her mind churned with the thoughts of meeting the Bondmaster. What if he thought she was an escaped slave? She could be executed.

'Is he a kind or a cruel man?'

'We will be going to the back of his house. Jin the kitchen slave will meet us there.'

Jenna did not feel relieved as she felt Ru Li had avoided answering her. She took her shawl and wrapped it around her head to conceal herself as much as possible.

Ru Li handed her one of the urns. She took it.

The road rose steadily in a sweeping bend until the last few paces when it steepened. Jenna's chest wheezed slightly at the exertion. She could feel the milk sloshing from one side to the other. With every step her chest seemed to constrict in rising panic that the man who dwelt in this house would not let her leave. Hurry with the boat Yan.

A large verandah of marble columns continued all around the house. The windows reached the full length of the walls from the roof to the stone porch. In the arch of each were stained glass designs. Inside could be seen white lace curtains hung in elegant scallops.

'How would you build such a house?' Jenna whispered.

'The master's father brought it with him when he settled. Some of it was hewn from the rocks in the hills as well.'

Suddenly a man with long black hair tied in a plait at the back darted from a doorway where the verandah ended.

He bowed to Ru Li and to Jenna. He didn't speak and didn't seem to think Jenna was strange. He took out a small pouch, gave it to Ru Li and then scurried off back into the house with the two urns.

Ru Li gestured for them to leave. As Jenna walked past the windows again she looked more closely at the stained glass pictures. Some were of rolling landscapes while others had children playing around an old woman on a porch.

'Jenna, come. He is slow to anger but would not like to be disturbed by people like us. Especially not today.'

Jenna began to walk but was unable to pull her eyes away from the windows. As she passed each one her neck craned closer and each one merged making it look like they were moving.

When they reached the hut Jenna sat down panting. Her mind was filled with the images of the stained glass windows. They looked so real; almost as if she could step into them and begin living again.

'What is the matter Jenna?' Ru Li handed Jenna some water in a ladle.

'Some memories came back to me from a long time ago. I might go and see how Yan and Kim are going.' She handed the empty ladle back to Ru Li and hurried out the door.

She didn't look at the house but could feel it staring back at her clutching at her memories. Know who built me pounded in her head.

Suddenly she saw her transport to freedom sitting proudly in the water. Yan and Kim stood looking at their masterpiece. Kim tested the steadiness of the mast. Yan slapped Kim on the back in recognition of the craftsmanship. They turned as they heard Jenna approaching. They both beamed at her.

'Jenna the gum is almost set. You can bid us farewell tomorrow. But tonight I think we will celebrate the beauty of the boat and our guest who made it happen. Kim will join us.'

Kim grunted as he had sat hunched again fussing where the mast was dovetailed into the hull.

'I have some tobacco left if you have the pipe.' Kim nodded in agreement.

Jenna looked at the newly restored vessel and wanted to sail away in it that moment.

'I will leave on the dawn. Thank you both for doing this.'

'Soon, soon, be patient slave.' She uttered.

Walking back to the hut the storm that had threatened earlier had passed allowing the day to brighten just a little. Ru Li was inside. There was some stew boiling away. Inside the pot Jenna saw meat joints, probably goat she thought. It had been a long time since she had tasted fresh meat.

Ru Li sat with the pouch Jin had given her opened on the reed mat. The pouch was full of pearls and polished stones and crystals. She had some bright yellow cloth and was stitching small gems onto it. The cloth looked like silk. Jenna had not seen such finely spun material for decades.

'What do you know of your master?'

Something was familiar about the pattern of the embroidery but she couldn't think why she would know it.

'You have been bonded in your life Jenna. You know it is not wise to know too much about your master. He is a kind man to answer your first question. But he is still a Bondmaster and must be obeyed. He does not interfere much in our lives, only when it is necessary if an offence is made against the rules his ancestor set down.'

'I am sorry to ask. My master was not kind and my life changed a great deal.'

'Yes we can see it in your eyes. Like the hare that runs free from the hunters trap; strong with the desire for freedom but broken from the pain endured to gain it. Kim and Yan will repair the boat very well. It will be strong and sturdy for your journey home.'

Jenna nodded.

'Rest while you can Jenna.'

She smiled at Ru Li's thoughtfulness. Leaning against the wall the memory of her grandmother knitting came to her as she watched Ru Li work her beauty with the needle into the cloth. Jenna was reciting her times tables and Kat was skipping and Jack was hitting a ball up against a half collapsed brick wall. It was the remains of the old home originally built on the land. Kat's dress was beautiful in the sunlight as was Jenna's. Her grandmother had found the material in a chest and made them one each.

The cloth and its pattern reminded her of the last night before she left her grandmother and later Gabriel as well. She had kept the pretty smock and turned it into a tablecloth. When she had finally left the old woman it had been the first thing she had packed. On that last night before her expulsion Gabriel had spilt some wine on it during their final meal together. The Purgers had torn it from her hands. It had been with her from the days of her childhood and as a young woman.

'What are you making Ru Li? It is very beautiful.'

'I am making an apron for the Bondmaster's daughter. She died a few days ago and this will be her burial dress.'

'Oh, that is old culture to shroud the dead in things so beautiful. That is sad.'

'She was a sickly girl that never came down to the village. I saw her once when I took milk there. She sat upon the verandah in a chair with blankets around her.'

'There are no children here either Ru Li?'

'No, only a few live to see themselves marry and bear their own. Come to the ceremony today Jenna.'

Jenna didn't answer. She didn't want to. She remembered the old ceremonies how decorated and festive they were and how morbid as well. Those traditions lasted long after they had any real meaning from the days when hope still existed. When there was still something to find beyond the horizon she thought to herself and the grief of losing it was a luxury.

They sat in silence the rest of the morning as Ru Li finished the embroidery. The apron looked stunning in its finery and intricate beading. What is the point thought Jenna. It will lie under the ground with no one to see it. But then what is the point of this journey you make slave echoed in her head.

The day meandered in semi gloom. The sounds of people gathering drifted into the hut. Jenna wrapped her scarf around her head and peeked outside the door. The villagers followed a cart draped in wreaths made from reed stalks. Some had centres of coloured stones breaking the monotony of the khaki straw. Inside was a small lump. Jenna could just make out the shape of feet. The Bondmaster walked behind in a fine suit. He was thin and tall and wore a great straw hat. His face remained hidden. The grey blonde ponytail hung down his back.

Jenna saw Ru Li join the villagers as the procession came past the hut. Ru Li went to the Bondmaster and offered the apron. The funeral cart stopped as the dainty piece was placed over the body. Ru Li stepped back into the crowd.

Jenna suddenly felt very sad for the little girl and the master. The brightness of the yellow lifted the gloom of the day and occasion but it also seemed lonely in its happiness. She decided to follow. Making sure her face was fully concealed she joined in the very back of the procession. It wound up through the village in a snake and towards the hill that had been hidden by the mansion. Amongst the scattered rocks and bushes Jenna could see a small area fenced off in a square shape with striking white slabs sticking out of the ground.

The cart pulled up near the little cemetery and the villagers naturally formed a circle around the gravesite.

The body of the child was lifted up and reverently placed into the open grave. No one sobbed; it had happened too often. The Bondmaster stood at the foot of the child's grave and spoke a prayer. Jenna heard every word and knew it so well she almost muttered it out loud.

'Ashes to ashes and dust to dust. Glory be to the father son and Holy Ghost. May Mary Louise Tenebrae rest in peace.'

Jenna stopped breathing as the sound of the child's name echoed through her mind. Tenebrae and Louise had been the name of the Tenebrae Matriarch. She wanted to run. She didn't want to know who the Bondmaster was. She wanted to be on her boat sailing with her heart full of the hope of getting to Gabriel.

I have to leave she thought. I will set sail tonight. I will risk the mast being weak. I can repair it in Singapore.

The crowd began to break up. She saw a large group of villagers coming towards her. She decided to mingle and walk with them. Suddenly she felt a hand on her arm. She stopped. Panic rose in her chest. Turning she saw it was Ru Li. Jenna's mouth was so dry that her tongue could not move.

'We will go home now. It was beautiful, wasn't it Jenna?'

Jenna nodded still not able to speak. Her mind and heart raced against each other. She wanted to run. She followed Ru Li down the hill in a daze.

Sitting in the hut she almost collapsed.

'Are you alright Jenna? It has upset you.' She gave Jenna a ladle with water.

Jenna gulped it down.

'I think I just want to leave. I have far to go. And I fear time is running out.'

Ru Li looked at Jenna.

'Time is running out Ru Li do you understand that. There will be no more time as we understand it. No memory of it or understanding. Nothing.'

'We will all die Jenna. That is what must happen to us all.'

Jenna didn't speak anymore. She lay down and closed her eyes.

The day grew dim quickly leading to the night. Her mind reeled with the sound of the child's name. Her name. Instead of curious surprise though, she was filled with fear. An indelible certainty that yet another wall was building to stop her leaving; this time it was her past. She would never get back to him; to her beloved Gabriel. She felt the leather pouch on her skin. It was still safe. Surely that meant something.

Yan and Kim returned in a good mood. Their hands were still covered in the black gum used to seal the boat.

'Your vessel is ready Jenna.' She noticed Yan slurred his words slightly and was unsteady on his feet.

'We have begun the celebrations already on your behalf.' He and Kim sat down laughing.

'I am grateful to you both so much for your kindness and hospitality. I had almost forgotten what that was until I came here.'

Kim poured Ru Li and Jenna a cup of the fermented goat's milk. It was strong and very sour. Jenna gagged on it but drank it out of politeness.

'A toast to our honoured guest.' chorused Yan. All four mugs made a dull thud against one another. The night progressed with revelry. It helped dull her fear at the image of another leash being tied around her neck; her family this time instead of Adrik.

Jenna woke with a fright. She had fallen asleep with everyone else. Yan snored and Kim lay propped up against the wall with an empty jug dangling from his hand. Ru Li was curled up on her mattress. She got up quietly. Going outside she gathered her sack and swag. It was lighter than expected. It was the moon. She had not seen it in many months but tonight it was almost full with the ash cloud gone it was like a beacon. She walked quickly to the boat. It stood like a dutiful servant waiting to set sail. Her head pounded slightly from the milk but her thoughts were clear.

She untied the rope and threw her things into the hull. Just as she was about to step in she heard footsteps.

'It is indeed a beautiful night to set sail. I haven't seen the moon so bright for most of the year.'

Jenna's heart stopped upon hearing the cultured voice which seemed so familiar. She straightened up.

'Yes it is.' was all she could think to say.

'I had heard the villagers talking of a guest arriving and was curious about it. It is not often we have travelers down our way. The large ports and bays are further to the south and the road on the high plateaus more direct.'

'I am sorry if I have trespassed into your village. I became lost after I was set free but I know where I am now and can continue my way. Again I am sorry if I have intruded.'

'Not at all. People are free to come and go as they please.'

He didn't move. Jenna stood waiting.

'If it is not rude I will take my leave. I would like to make it to the Bay of Singapore to restock.'

'I am Jackson Johannes Tenebrae. I am the Bondmaster here as was my father before me. I am pleased that our village has been hospitable to you. My grandmother always spoke of kindness being important even in the most desperate of times. It's what stops the degradation taking complete hold and life being reduced to barbarism.'

Jenna nearly collapsed as she heard her brother speak. The memory of her grandmother's voice reciting that mantra over and over again bloomed in her mind. Jack, it was her brother Jack.

Her heart wanted to break in two. So this is where her father had gone and Jack had followed; all those years ago when they had disappeared from her life with no word. A great longing to hug him and stay and tell him who she was swelled inside her to the point of making her choke. But as she gathered her breath to speak the pouch moved against her breast and scratched her flesh. It was like a reminder that it had not been her family that had sustained her will to live over the decades but what lay inside the pouch. Finally gathering herself she replied.

'It is a pleasure to meet you Jackson Johannes Tenebrae. And your grandmother seems to be a wise woman for this is the first kindness and warmth I have felt for a long time. I am also sorry as I believe it was your daughter that was buried today.'

'Yes it was. I take young wives in the hope that they may give me children to perpetuate my family name. But the days grow dimmer every year. I fear that time has finally run out. It is a blessing that the children no longer survive for there is nothing to offer them anymore.'

'I agree it is a blessing. Now I will leave you and hope that your gentleness will follow me to the next place.'

Jack nodded and stepped away. Jenna hoisted the sail. It instantly caught the cool breeze. The boat glided out smoothly into the bay.

'I would like to walk to the heads as you leave for it is a beautiful sight to watch a boat sail in the moonlit ocean. On the dawn I will paint it on the window of the house as another memory of my life.'

Jenna nodded as thick sorrowful tears ran down her cheeks. She saw the figure of her brother walk along the cliff. As she gathered momentum and broke out into the full ocean she heard his voice call out.

'What is your name traveler so I may place it on my window pane?'

'My name is Jenna Louise Tenebrae.'

She watched the dwindling figure stop suddenly as the words met him. He then started to wave to her.

'Finish your part of the Tenebrae story Jack. Paint it into your dainty windows for what it is worth.'

She heard his voice fade behind her imploring her to come back. She began to sob as the boat sailed with purpose disappearing into the beauty of the glistening moonlit waves.

3 Letter Eight

As I sit at the foot of the old man's tomb and watch the stone crumble, I search my memories and still find you there. I scored the path I trod in those early days through the deserts and mountains into my flesh, so I would always know the way back to you. I knew the loftiness of these cliffs peering across the vastness of time would always bring hope and never let love die. It was why I decided to remain in this place.

The stone of our beloved city sculpted the first words of our history together and now this implacable granite of the mountain chisels the beginning of the end.

It was the death of the old man which heralded the first rays of the sun to not reach us; the birth of an eternal darkness. His memory lingers as vividly as yours. His words were wise and gentle and true. They are food that replenishes my mind with stoic patience. I grieve for him and for you. That is all the grief I shall allow in this fractured life. I sit here at his grave with his voice echoing in my mind just like your love clamors in my heart.

I am on the other side of the world from where you lie. The winters become harsher and the mountain will no longer give shelter from the wretched cold. It is time to seek out another place. I am not welcome here and the earth tells me it is time to endure its ravages once more. I have taken my fill and have glutted on my sorrow and the fear of deciding my own fate. The story of my end is nearing. I have not taken my punishment but remain hidden from judgment. It is time to choose a master in a land where my body can be nourished. Not only will I have redemption for my willful life when so many others must walk with gaoled dreams and unimagined purpose I will grow strong again to make my naïve hope real.

I am coming dear heart

The terrible rage of the waves grew with the increasing darkness. Jenna's arms burned and her hands slipped as the blisters kept breaking mixing her blood with the saltwater. The little boat did what she asked of it as she guided the rudder.

Another tyrannical wall of water loomed before her. It was so steep a boulder of fear sat in her stomach as the hull of the boat climbed its way up. It teetered on the brink of the wave before racing down the slip face. The momentum gained from each climb helped ease the burden on the little boat as it approached the next behemoth of the ocean.

The rudder wrenched her arm away from her as a squall pummeled the left side. As the water thumped the deck it spun the boat around so that she now faced towards the Bay of Singapore. For a moment she thought of Jack on the cliff. How easy would it be to return to him? She would be welcome there.

'Oh dear heart, I do this for you and no other.' she screamed as the fear and terror of the night engulfed her. She gripped the oars and heaved to make the boat turn.

'Heave Jenna, heave again.' She yelled into the storm.

'Heave, hea…..' the water drenched her. Losing the grip of the oar she flailed and tried to suck in air as the salt water washed down her throat.

Coughing she found the mast and clung to it to catch her breath. Wave after wave of the ocean struck and pounded her little boat as if in punishment for trying to live when the writ of death for the earth had been issued. Earth and her mighty oceans would not survive so how dare she?

'You won't stop me. Nothing has so far and you won't either. There are no tears to give you. You may have my fear of not finishing what began so many years ago but there is no fear of my death at your hands. I have seen the anguish of those you choose to consume in your mighty bosom. I have seen those who flee their persecution and the cauldrons of desperation that became their eyes as they clung to sides of the slave ships. I have felt their hands claw at my flesh as they were wrenched into your hateful depths. But I will not give in to your tantrum. I will not succumb to your frenzied desire to suck the flesh off my body. I will give you no satisfaction. We both know that these are the end days for all. But my time has not come yet, just like yours. Be calm and let us both watch those days come to their fullness. Give those of us left the last imprint of your beauty not your ugly rage as the memory that we will die with. Let the last days be dignified. Let the last days be full of kindness. Let the last days be moments of peace and happiness.

You have watched the children of your sandy shores and rocky cliffs spill their blood and tear their flesh in vanity and pride. They have warred and loved and paid homage to their history with you and the earth as witness. You once let them be your master as they grew in strength and knowledge so that only your most terrible rages could diminish their questing hearts. Great iron ships that could withstand your lashes without even leaving a scar on their hides.

Until the master of us, the one that burns your horizon like ours, decided that things will no longer live and we were thrust from our towers of vanity back to your heaving arms and cries of sorrow. So now let us be friends to each other and not be remembered as legends of madness and monsters.

If you will not cradle like a mother with her child then hurl me through the smoke and ash to see the stars shining upon your heaving bosom.

If you must thrust me down then make it on the lands that will lead me back to my heart's hope.

There is nothing more to conquer.

Give me these things and you will have won the love of a soul, a gift more precious than broken flesh and bone.'

Jenna's voice drifted across the emptiness down one wave and heaving up the next. Her litany sucked into the maelstrom. Suddenly she felt the rudder go slack. The rain stopped. She sat and waited. She wiped the water and salt scale from her face.

The blanket of dark began to brighten a little. She took out some white beans and let them soften in the salt water. She chewed them. Traded for the sacks of grain they had no taste. The howl of the wind had dimmed and only the low hush of the eye of the storm surrounded her.

'You see I would cry for my brother but not out of fear of you. I have forsaken the chance to live my last days in comfort with my family. I cry because of this journey that began so long ago, its purpose has almost crumbled to dust. But I will not cry now as you tease me with this false hope of quiet. I know you simply wait to re-gather.'

She stared into the abyss around her thinking of Jack. It was the last day of the great harvest. Grandmother stood in the paddock with a dozen sheaves around her. Jack was lying next to her on a tied bundle of reeds.

'I love this the most Grandmother.'

'What's that Jackson?'

'This.'

'You know this will not be your last harvest.'

'I know but it is the best it will ever be for me. I won't ever be happier any more than I am now.'

'There will be more happiness Jackson.'

'Nope there won't be. There will be more memories, events and experiences but there won't be more happiness.'

'Don't ever stop trying to find more though.'

Jenna remembered the warning look on the face of their grandmother; half admonishing him for relegating the rest of his life as if it was an afterthought.

'Where are you going Jack?' Jenna had asked

'I don't know. It's part of the rules now. Once we are old enough we have to leave.'

'But you must have some idea? I mean even I know that I would like to go to Paris one day.'

Jenna remembered the look between Jack and Grandmother.

'Well I guess you are one of the lucky ones.'

'Come over here Jen. I need you to lift these bundles.' called Grandmother.

So her question had been answered. Jenna knew now why he had never answered her. He had been chosen along with Kat to be with the Bondmasters. What a life she thought. Who drew the straws to say who became chartered and bound to rule and others to serve. Who drew the straw in her family? She now knew what happened to her father but her mother was barely remembered and it was still unknown where her final resting place came to be.

Her mind jumped to the last day she had seen Jack. He had his rucksack on his back and was wearing his straw hat. It was the same shape as the one he was wearing at the village. Truly he did not let go of his last moments of happiness either. She had run up to him. He was only a few years older but seemed like he had already lived an age. She noticed that his face looked worn and he had dark circles under his eyes as if he had not slept all night.

'Jack have you got plenty of water.'

'Yes Grandmother.'

He stooped and looked at Jenna.

'I don't know what to tell you but one day you will see how it all works. One part of me wants to tell you to follow your heart Jen but the other wants me to tell you to do as you are asked. In the end it will be the difference between giving some kindness back into the world or forsaking it all together just to satisfy a selfish desire.'

'I won't ever see you again will I?'

'I don't think so. And it maybe if we do run into one another we won't be able to see each other as family.'

'I would never do that to you or Kat or Grandmother. What is the point of everything we have read and been taught if we cannot even do that?'

Jack hesitated.

'I am not so sure that I would even if the chance allowed for us to meet again.'

Jenna pulled away from him in anger and disgust at his answer.

Kat had said the same thing when she had left and her heart had hardened even more with Jack's departure. She would always know there were things more deserving then unthinking devotion to duty.

'Don't be angry with me. You will understand. Be careful what you choose Jen. Sometimes a dream isn't worth the price you pay to make it happen; remaining hungry can mean more in the end than finding a stale piece of bread to feast upon.'

Her heart sank along with the boat as it dipped and bobbed on the calming ocean. Should she go back? It would be her last chance for refuge. It had been so long since she had first trod those cobble stone streets that made her legs ache and twist her ankles. Would anything still remain? She searched for the coast but it was still out of sight. Maybe Jack was right. Her heart still swelled with anger at his words to her. It was only in these last moments that he would break the oath he had taken to seek reunion with his sister. Did you ever think to look for me or Kat or make sure Grandmother was safe in her last days? I was the one who forsook my Bondmasters duty to stay with the old woman as she lay dying. It was the least I could offer her; more than your pretty decorations on windows in poor imitation of your happiest moments. Jack if you were unwilling to extend a kind thought or action before your hand was forced then all that homage to our grandmother is meaningless.

Jenna began to feel drowsy as the gentle rocking eased her anger and racing thoughts.

The blue door came to her mind. She saw the ancient brass knocker perched majestically in the centre. It was the cast image of a blazing sun with a smile on its face. It seemed to mock now rather than warmly greet the visitor. The door opened.

'Hello!' the face was antique with a patchy set of teeth that complimented every weathered crevice.

'Sit!'

'Thank you'

'What did you do today?'

'I went to the markets near the old cathedral. I bought some bread. I had forgotten the taste.'

She had taken the small brown lump of baked bread and placed it on the table. His face beamed at her like the sun on the door. The throaty laugh at her minute joy relaxed her. Her heart slowed.

'Some wine?'

'Yes please.'

The taste was sharp like vinegar; spoilt by too long in the bottle. She read the faded label; Alsace Grand Cru Riesling.

'Where did you find it?'

'In a cellar that I stumbled upon while I was excavating.'

She could barely swallow the second mouthful it was so bitter.

'Good eh!'

She snorted at his comment. She spat the liquid back into the glass.

'If only the world was this perfect. We could enjoy the simple act of sharing bread and wine together. But now it must be one or the other and only when it is allowed.'

They toasted their glasses and threw the remains of the wine onto the swept floor. It stained some rubble that lay in the corner. Her fingers stung where the vinegar spilt into the small cuts on her hands. She had worked all day in the pits just to buy the bread. Every mouthful was worth it.

'I came here to see what a statue of thinking looked like.'

'And have you seen it?'

'Not yet. I think it is ruined and lies amongst these stones that we move.'

'We will look for it another day. The wall is almost built. There will be a moment for ourselves.'

They toasted their empty glasses again and ate the rest of the bread. As they lay down together her body shivered with joy and fear. How amongst mindless destruction does this happen?

'Do you remember the statue?'

'Which one?'

'The one I was talking about.'

'I remember many.'

'To know more than one must be wonderful.'

She closed her eyes as his breath moved over her and her back stretched out onto the marble floor. Holding her tightly his touch was delicate and firm, like she imagined the hand of the sculptor would be like as he carved the statue into existence.

'Please don't ever let me go.' She pleaded as she released her body onto his.

Suddenly Jenna felt the boat lurch as the wave slammed the side. She braced herself as another one pummeled her. The force shook the memories from her mind completely as the storm front gathered before her. Jenna smiled as its mouth consumed her and the little boat.

'You woke again just as my memories woke from their sleep. But you are too late for the flame of hope has been rekindled. You should never have slept for I have been granted ointment for my wearied bones and torn flesh and I am ready to stand you down.'

She thought of his face and his body, his warmth and his love and knew that nothing would stop her. She knew then that there was a chance of a life for her, even just for a few moments. Some things must remain sacred even when god has been disproven or forgotten. The stale bread is worth the price we pay she thought to herself. Jack had lost his courage to live. He chose bondage to a set of rules over his own desires. What an empty well to draw upon as the dark days grow longer.

Grandmother was right. More happiness can be found you just need to keep searching for it.

Jenna looked into the black clouds that were so low that the waves appeared to lick them. A cliff of water formed in front of her. She knew the little gift of Kim and Yan would not survive. She tied the sacks of beans to her legs and then herself to the mast.

'Thank you Yan and Ru Li. You were kind before it was ever asked for or needed. I forgive you Jack. Dear heart I am coming.'

Jenna braced herself.

'I see you have not heard me either mighty mother and would rather condemn yourself to rage and loathing. You cannot cleanse the fatal wound that lies in the heart of the sun. Your bitterness consumes you woman but it will not destroy me.'

Jenna felt the water thrust her down. The sound of the wood splintering amongst the roar of the hurricane belied the tenacious hope that sat in her heart. Another fist of water punched her down into the choleric seas but each time the mast speared through the surface allowing her to breath.

In the blackness the seething clouds glared at the ragdoll being tossed around. No cries of terror came from the lonely figure, only defiance as solid as the mast that buoyed her; her unfailing belief that she would survive this torment as well, never dimmed amongst the turmoil of the storm.

Suddenly a window of light broke the dark. Its insolent radiance revealed the yellow crescent of a beach. The waves rolled her over and over again pushing her away from them towards the sand as if they did not know what to do with this creature that neither feared nor loved them and could not be destroyed.

Jenna roused slightly and looked at the desert stretching ahead in smiling undulations. Inside her shirt she could feel the pouch safely tucked away near her heart.

'I am coming dear heart.' She whispered as her head fell onto the soft grains of the beach.

4 Letter Seven

I search the horizon through foggy and aged eyes. I am still in Old China. The old man eventually passed. I counted he lived 110 years. They mourned him for a long time and revered him. I wept bitterly over his death. The last burial I remember that cried for the sacredness of life was my grandmother's.

I wanted to come home to you and end all of this; I wanted my longing to be satisfied and the story be finished. I wanted to see the paved roads and ruined stones of the ancient palaces that testified to the human who woke each day with the promise that things would never end. When there was all the time under the sun to seek out what could lay beyond the dawn.

I want to hear your heart and feel your breath and listen to your words again. I have had enough of wandering and begging for a silhouette of life.

Too often the venomous whisper of why didn't you follow enters my dreams only to wake me and hurl me back into this dark and lonely existence.

But then I remember you did try but they would not let you leave just like they wouldn't let me stay.

I float like a dead body in the ocean after a storm, no direction and no hope and no memory of how it happened. I was called an intruder and ripped from the very mortar that joined my flesh and bones. The Great Purge they called it and to what end? I overheard a merchant one day. He spoke about how the great walls that surrounded the city which held you captive had fallen. I remember him laughing at the stupidity of people. To think that guns and bulwarks of iron and wire would stop anything. They don't understand the time they are living in he had said. They live in the past when those things mattered. When the other side had something to fight for as well but no one has anything now, so drawing lines in the sand is futile.

I left the merchant with such vitriol in my heart that the bile rose in my throat as I thought of the decades lost. Then I remembered the words you whispered to me 'It will not be allowed yet for you and me to end. Only at the very last when all other plans and deeds of the masters has been accomplished will we see our hopes and desires made real. Our prison lies in their blind arrogant rule; rules embedded in our coded flesh.'

I threw a small posy of herbs and wild daisies on the tomb of the old man. The sun held him close and he radiated its nascent wisdom until it became too weak to keep him alive. He never spoke of sorrow or pain and would not understand mine. He knew the truths of the world and accepted them gladly. Unlike those despots who tore me away from you; they thought they saw a new horizon beyond the sun but they were fooled for they ran out of bullets and the walls they built fell also.

I am coming dear heart

'Wake up.'

The staff struck Jenna's back. It touched a badly bruised rib. The pain shot through her like a knife. She tried to get up but something held her down.

'Wake up!' spoke the voice again along with another bolt of agony from the prodding stick.

'Untie me.' Her tongue was swollen and her throat felt like it was full of razor blades.

Rough hands yanked at the ropes binding her to the mast. She rolled over and suddenly felt sick. Her chest wheezed in rhythm with the throbbing in her bones.

'Do you have some water?'

'A little.' A few drops landed on her mouth. They evaporated in an instant. More came.

Her saviour sat her up.

'I have hurt my chest. I don't think I can walk.'

'Augustus can carry you.'

She looked at the mast still in one piece from where it had splintered from the hull of the boat. She saw the sack of beans. They had spilled out the top. It was so bright she blinked painfully from the glare of the sand. She looked at the sky. The darkness of the storm had gone but the grey film that now shrouded the world remained but seemed to magnify the yellow beach.

'Who are you? Why is it so bright?'

Her mind tried to make sense as it cleared. Where was she? Who was this man helping her? She watched the man taste one of the beans and spit it out.

'They are ruined. Full of salt. Between the sand and the sea we would both become preserved nomads. I am Quentus and this is Augustus.'

Jenna looked and saw the massive creature. She had seen trains of them moving across the deserts of northern Africa all those years ago. They were called camels. She remembered their name from tablets her grandmother had read to her. Quentus' black weathered face contrasted against the desert. He had a cloth wrapped around his head but she could just see the line of dark hair. His eyes were almost black and looked at her furtively not wanting to make contact with hers.

'I am Jenna. Thank you for helping me Quentus. Where am I?'

'On the coast of Persia.'

She let out an inaudible sigh of relief. So mighty and fearsome ocean instead of conquering me you threw me in the direction of my heart's desire. Be as kind to the next one who dares tread your stormy paths and pleads their litany of salvation she thought.

'The desert seems to stretch further then I remember it.' Her eyes searched across the dunes.

'How long since you have seen these lands?'

'Many years.'

'Persia is the name given to lands between the old tribal fiefdoms of Judea and Egypt. There is no sea that separates them. The desert is so vast now that it is almost impossible to cross it from here.'

She hesitated. She hadn't thought the memories from her first exiled trek would be obliterated by the ever changing earth. She looked at the remains of the boat sitting on the beach and then the camel. It snorted and spat on the sand behind her. She needed food and water to continue. She would not survive such a long journey without help.

'Am I able to travel north from here?'

'I can guide you some of the way.'

'I have nothing to give in payment.'

'My journey goes north as well. It will not be any burden to take you some of the way.'

Augustus let out a groan as his master forced him to sit down.

Even sitting the beast towered over her. On either side it was saddled with tools and bags of goods made in the universal reed cloth. When Jenna pressed against them it felt like beans in one and flour in the others. Her sides screamed with pain as she hoisted herself up onto the hump of Augustus.

'Now hang on. We follow the beach for a day then turn inland.'

Jenna nearly lost her grip as the camel rose up with no grace. She nodded barely registering his words as the blooms of pain increased with each lurching movement.

As they ambled along the coastline she looked at the black water. It stretched for miles. The ocean was calm with barely any waves crashing into the lips of the beach. The jaundiced sand made more stunning by the malignant stillness of the waves. She wondered how long before the remains of her little boat would be washed away and forgotten; and along with it Jack, Ru Li and Yan.

The terror from the storm welled suddenly inside. How had she survived it? How had she survived all these years? She felt her breast; the pouch sat safely tucked away. She remembered the words miracle, fate and destiny. She remembered how dramatic they seemed in the stories she read about them. But what other explanation was there? A decision was made, it may be judged whether it was a rational choice or not but either way she had been made it. Mountains may have needed to be crossed, great storms of the ocean needed to be defeated but she had made it this far. The world was hostile in its death throes and offered no protection for her heart's desire. Surely it was fate on her side.

Quentus walked alongside her humming a tune. She closed her eyes feeling more in rhythm with the strides of Augustus. She began to doze lightly.

'Here! Look! You can see the fist and the large head. It is all that appears to remain.'

'At least there is something.'

She placed her own hand over the great sculpted hand. It was bronze. For some reason she thought it would be stone.

'I wish I lived when this was made. Imagine what it must have been like to make new things and see them age into posterity.'

She had tried to imagine the hammer bashing the metal into shape. She wondered if the sinews of the massive arms were molded from the sculptor's own form. The head when it was cast; what thoughts were locked inside never to escape?

'It is this statue that heralded man's great grief at the sun's death Gabriel. We could see our own death and understood what would be lost. As each day dawned with its veil of misery or happiness with every age of man we learnt to see the signs and try to change what lay behind the veil. It was for this reason this statue should remain as it reflects the grief that had consumed the hearts of men. It is the grief I feel about my life. Seeing what lies ahead and not wanting it and not being able to change it. We think therefore we are. Who had said that?'

'Ancient words beloved, from a man called Descartes. It's what made us feel culpable until we realized it isn't our decision at all. We are only parts of something larger. But it is our minute desires that define us, not the grand rubric of the universe. Its indifference and our sincerity is the great paradox of our existence.'

She gripped Gabriel's hand feeling comforted by his words. It lifted some of the shadow of confusion about whom she was and why she felt so driven to see the old city of Paris and learn of the age antiquity. To have her desires fulfilled. It was this that made the humans now different to their ancestors and what made her feel apart from the world she was born into.

The arm of the statue ended in a jagged piece of metal. The great fist that would have rested under the chin was still intact. It was in the ruins of the old capital. It had become the forbidden part of the city but they had risked it none the less because of all the buried treasures of history that lay here.

'I want what they had. I want the luxury of knowing that even if every question had not been answered that at some point in time they would be.'

Gabriel moved away and began to rummage through another pile of stone and detritus.

'Another by the great artist Rodin!' his voice echoed in the stillness of the ruins. She held her breath waiting for someone to come and evict them from their treasure hunt.

He strode over with a beaming smile and a dusty piece of metal.

'Miss Jenna, behold the old woman of winter. It's magnificent in its detail and sorrow. Doesn't it make you feel the sibilant chill of a cold day?'

Jenna took it in her hands. She polished the dust off and saw the intricate decrepitude of the withered figure. Yes that is what it is like when the long nights come and there is no more sunlight to warm you. Again what vision brought this figure into creation? The aching need for warmth and light so seminal for them to live; so exquisitely drawn in the disfigured statue. How would the artist have seen what would become of those who walked after him?

'Yes beloved. It speaks truthfully and with clarity that words would only diminish in their clumsiness.'

'So you have seen what thinking looks like and the old woman of winter.'

'Thank you Gabriel. What happened here? The buildings remain but all this beauty is destroyed.'

'A war many generations ago between the Bondmasters and the bonded; the war of the Charter. It decided nothing and neither side gained anything. Many pieces of art and the objects that told our history were destroyed by both sides to stop reminding them of what they had lost. The buildings gave shelter but the art and the decorations if they couldn't be burned for fuel were broken down to make weapons. I am surprised that these remain. They could be melted down for Purgers arrows the bronze is so thick. It was as if fate held onto them until you could see them Jenna Louise Tenebrae.' His face broke into a huge smile.

'Take it!'

'No it would not be right. It should stay here along with the others. These remnants are the artist's legacy and epitaph telling the world the incorrigible strength of beauty and our lost history.'

She placed the statue back down next to the large head and fist. She buried them beneath the gravel until there was no trace.

'I don't want anyone to take them. They belong here. Who knows perhaps a miracle will happen and the sun won't die after all and this can all happen again.' She patted her hands free of dust.

'I think we should leave in case the patrols return.'

He had walked up to her silently. He wiped the dust from her face and took it in both hands and kissed her passionately.

'I think we see more beyond the horizon then anything this artist saw. Nothing can take this away for even as the ray of the last dawn reaches us, all it will do is destroy the flesh and not the will that sustains us. Tell me how any of this matters at this moment. Lifeless objects that captured a thought of one man's view of the world. Perhaps he never knew the happiness and joy that we have; surely that alone would cause those withered crevices of the old woman to swell with life again.'

She had stared into his eyes and knew this was her grave and this moment their headstone; their love for each other their defining epitaph. The melancholy that the statues had caused lifted with his words and touch.

'I will spend the rest of my life with you Gabriel and eternity beyond it. This is my home where I will let my bones rest.'

Suddenly pain shot through her. She woke panting. Blinking she found herself lying on sand again.

'You fell Jenna. I think you had fallen asleep.'

'Oh my chest Quentus. I need something to bind it.'

Quentus undid one of the cloths that had been placed on Augustus back as a saddle.

'This should do.'

'Lift your arms.' He commanded.

He slid the reed clothe underneath her back and wrapped it firmly around her chest and breasts. After the initial stab of pain her breathing became easier.

'Up onto Augustus again. We are heading into the desert now. Here is some water.'

This time she kept looking into the endless dunes.

'I will tell you something about me Quentus if you will tell me your story. Is that fair?'

'Only if you wish.

'I have been bonded for these last few years and I am making my way back home; most likely to die.'

'Hmm, like all of us. I am still bonded and am bringing supplies back.'

'Is your Bondmaster difficult?'

'Hmm no. Have you been bonded your whole life?'

'No.'

'I have. But I have not lived as long as you.'

She smiled slightly at his comment about her age. She had only seen blurred images of herself in water and wondered what she must look like now.

'You are a kind man to help me like this.'

'Perhaps, but then you don't really know me and you must be a trusting person to follow me. It is not uncommon for one bonded to seek another to replace them to gain their freedom.'

Jenna didn't answer. But knew he was right. They didn't know one another. A massive dune rose before them. The incline was so steep that Jenna got off Augustus worried she would fall and began to scramble behind the two desert dwellers. Once on the top of the ridge she saw the inexorable vista of yellow extend until the horizon and back across the vague black outline of the ocean. The silence was palpable making her skin feel like it was being tickled but also stilled her mind at its constancy.

She got back up onto Augustus who spat in readiness for the final leg of the journey.

'Should it be hotter than this in the desert?'

'Yes I remember as a child we would not trek in the heat of the day but only in mornings and evenings. But now the sun is so weak that the desert is best travelled in daylight. The chill of the night would freeze a person now.'

'Yes I remember reading stories about the Berbers of Old Africa who lived in the great Sahara desert. They knew each grain of sand and how it would blow in the wind and which path to travel for safety. Are you descended from those people Quentus?'

'Perhaps. I was bonded as a child and do not know where I was born. Be careful of Augustus when he senses the end of the journey he sometimes breaks into a run. Hang on if he does because I will not be able to stop him.'

Sure enough just as Quentus finished speaking the camel lurched into a fast trot then a gallop following the ridge of the great sand dune. She saw on the horizon a small oasis begin to form and a structure amongst the trees.

'Augustus, slow down!' She barely held her grip on the reigns.

The camel did not respond but gathered pace. Nearing the island of palms a small pool revealed itself. It was black on its surface like the ocean. Augustus stopped suddenly to drink throwing Jenna off into the sand. Through the blur of agonised bolts of pain she heard the camel's indifferent greedy slurping. She giggled slightly at the sound. Getting her breath she realised how thirsty she was seeing the crystal purity of the water. She staggered over and drank like Augustus. It tasted earthy but revived her.

'Thank you Augustus, you're haste has relieved my thirst.'

She stood and saw Quentus coming down the slope of the last dune. He waved, happy to see they were both safe.

She turned and looked at her surroundings. The oasis extended for half a mile in every direction and in the middle of it she saw the ruins of a castle. Jenna calculated by the windows there were at least a dozen small rooms. There was one fully completed turret and one that looked as though it had collapsed to half its original height. She suddenly wondered if the Bondmaster could be watching from within the dark windows. She stood still near Augustus who had just finished drinking. Quentus arrived and washed in the water.

'Ahh.' He sighed 'It is good to be home.'

'Come inside.'

'What about Augustus?' Jenna asked.

'He will be fine. He will rest in the shade. This way.'

Jenna followed Quentus. An archway carved into the front wall revealed nothing beyond its entrance only a pitch black doorway. It swallowed Quentus as he walked inside.

Jenna's eyes took a long time to adjust in the darkness that engulfed her. It was cooler inside the walls of the building but its silence was not comforting like the desert. Further into the passage some light managed to break the thick walls. At the end she could see a courtyard. A stone table and bench sat in the middle. Quentus breezed past her with the sacks he had removed from Augustus. She walked into the open space and saw that it sat directly in the centre of the constructed walls. Twelve windows peered down into the space through mottled shade from a fig vine that grew across palm fronds.

'Sit Jenna.' He disappeared into one of the doors. She went to the table. She ran her hands over the smooth stone. She remembered her dream about Gabriel in the ruins of Paris.

Quentus placed a clay pitcher, a bowl of dates and some flat bread in front of her.

'It is not much but it is all I have. I managed to barter for some dried pork at the markets. It is soaking and will make a feast for a few days at least.'

'I will rest for today and may ask for some bread and dates and directions to the north coast of these lands. My journey has been a long one and I don't wish to prolong it anymore.'

'Yes of course.'

She poured some water into a clay bowl and sipped. It was fresh and cool. She took some of the bread and savoured every mouthful.

'Quentus please join me.' But he did not answer. He had left the courtyard.

She continued to eat. The silence penetrated. She kept looking at the dark slits of the windows above, checking to see if anyone watched her. She felt guilty at her unease. It was an insult to the generosity of Quentus and the salubriousness of the castle.

'Are you enjoying the dates? They were a treasure found along the way.'

Jenna jumped at the sudden sound of his voice.

'I went to see if the master had returned but he has not.'

'Is he expected soon?' Her stomach began to flutter as the sound of Adrik's voice flashed in her head.

'I don't know. I lose the time so easily. The sun is not reliable anymore and I have been busy with building.'

'What do you mean? Are you restoring the castle?'

'No building it. There was nothing here before only a tent.'

Jenna stopped eating, astounded at the work that it would have taken.

'May I take a look at the castle Quentus? My grandmother would often read stories of knights in castles in the days of antiquity.'

'Yes please do. This wing is the only finished section. But please eat your meal first. It will go to waste otherwise.'

'At least sit with me.'

'No I need to do many things. My journey took longer than expected.' He disappeared again.

She felt full quickly. This food was rich compared to beans and chaff. Jenna tried some of the dates. She could only eat one of them; their sweetness had long been forgotten.

Getting up she walked into the entrance that Quentus had come from and saw a stairway leading up to the next storey. It wound in a tight spiral. The stairs were almost too small for her feet to stand on. Arriving at the second level the corridor of stone stretched before her. On one side were the windows that looked down onto the courtyard and on the other were doors; each matching the windows in their spacing and number.

She looked at the first door and a feeling that something tantalizing was behind it struck her. Her hand rested on the latch unsure if she should enter. Unable to resist her curiosity she pulled the bolt free and stepped inside the room. It was bare except for a chest under a window which revealed the vista of the desert. She walked over to it and looked out. To her left she saw an area that had been excavated. Her shin bumped the chest sitting beneath the window. Opening it she could feel it was made from the reed material in a densely woven design. Inside it was empty, as if it had never been used.

Closing the door softly she stepped back into the corridor. It ended in a bricked up arch where the rest of the castle had not been finished. To her left was the last door. A square of light reflected onto the very centre of the dark timber. The light showed the beautiful texture of the grain. Jenna touched it to see if it was real. She wondered where it had come from. In the middle plank there was a small emblem carved into it. She opened the door not expecting anything. As she peered into the room her eyes were met with opulence and wealth that she had never seen before. The room was fully furnished. The bed was covered in richly embroidered cushions and layers of quilts. Red and gold curtains surrounded it as they hung elegantly from a hoop attached to the ceiling. Jenna saw two chests along the opposite wall beneath each of the windows. A magenta drape lazily caressed them as a breeze teased them. She touched the fine veil that overhung the bed. Her fingers had never felt such softness. The sumptuous bed seemed to seduce her so that she wanted to lie on it and sleep for an eternity. The colours overwhelmed her senses. She stood and looked out of the window. In the very far distance she could see the thin black line of the ocean in one direction and closer over to the left was the quarry. She bent down and opened one of the chests. It was full with more of the linen that lay on the bed. She picked up a folded sheet but as her fingers grasped it, it disintegrated. Gasping she pulled her hand away quickly. It must be so old. Things have not been made with silk for centuries now. Feeling guilty she closed the chest not wanting to ruin anything else.

She looked around the chamber. It was pristine in that there was no dust or anything out of place. But it also looked unoccupied for many years. She wondered about Quentus. Bondmasters were not allowed to leave their residences unless under exceptional circumstances. What had happened here?

She looked at the second chest and opened it. Inside were robes and jewelry and on the top lay two unopened scrolls. One had a red seal and the other a black one.

Her heart began to beat faster upon seeing the black seal. She closed the lid quickly shutting out the sight of the scrolls. She noticed that the day had begun to dim. It would be night again soon and she would be on her way tomorrow. It was not up to her to guide Quentus fate but to ensure her own came to its fullness.

She walked down the spiral stair case. She stopped at a tiny window and saw Quentus was placing some bricks into a cart.

'Hi ya, Quentus.' She called as she walked out of the building and towards him.

'Can I help you?'

'If you wish. I am trying to finish that row of bricks before the light goes completely.' Looking past him Jenna saw a partially constructed wall. She tried to pick up one of the bricks but the pain was too much.

'Perhaps you can mortar the stones as I place them.'

'Yes!' she wheezed

Brick after brick was laid and mortared into position. As the last of the day left the final stone was cemented into place.

'Thank you Jenna. Little by little the Keep gets finished.'

'I cannot believe you have built all this on your own Quentus.'

'Yes all of it. I can take my time with completing the rest of it as I made sure the first chamber was built to store everything for the master when he returns. Did you think his chamber was worthy?'

Jenna hesitated before answering, a little perturbed that he had known she had gone into the rooms.

'Perhaps you can tell me a bit of your story tonight as we eat.'

'I will fetch some water for us to wash in.' Quentus left.

Jenna made her way back to the courtyard. The chill air of the dry desert struck her. Her ribs throbbed from the work but it was bearable; she had felt worse in her life.

Quentus dropped a bucket of water near her. She stooped and first washed her face then her hands and arms. She noticed how calloused her hands had become; years of tilling the lands of Adrik and before then as a reed maiden. Her knuckles resembled the knots in the grain of timber of those doors above her.

Quentus chose to join her for a feast of dates and hommus and bread for this meal. He placed a fresh pitcher of water and bowls to drink from and sat opposite her.

'I will begin with my story Quentus. I volunteered to be bonded so that I could journey more easily back to the north where I will spend the last days of my life. I lived in Old China for many years but the winters were too harsh to cross the mountains that way. So I became bonded in the lands to the south. And now as an old woman I make way back to the only place I have ever called home.'

Quentus nodded.

'I have been a bonded servant to Sheik Adbul Mul Derab for as long as I can remember. He left here when this place was just a tent in an oasis. On the day he left he said to me, Quentus build me a castle to return to. Place everything I have in those chests in the rooms. As he rode off on his camel he never looked back. That would be years ago now.'

'He never explained where he was going or why?'

'No. But it does not matter for when he returns I can show him what I have been doing and he cannot beat me.'

'Was he a kind or a cruel master?'

'He was my master. What else is there to say?'

Jenna grimaced inwardly at the comment but conceded that it was the wrong question to ask. She had every choice and still had chosen to stay with Adrik.

'Was the time the Sheik left when the desert began to form the land bridge to Egypt?'

'Perhaps. I do not remember now.'

Jenna guessed the Sheik had seen a way to escape but she could not reconcile the cruelty of allowing Quentus to remain bonded when he had decided to forfeit his own vows.

'Can you read Quentus?'

'I can count for bartering and building the walls but that is all. I have no need of reading.'

Jenna nodded wondering whether to tell Quentus or not about the scrolls in the chest. Perhaps deep down like her there was a kernel of desire yet to be fulfilled to which only his soul was allowed to see. Perhaps all of this was just filling in time until the real living could be set free.

'Quentus I looked in the chests in the master's chamber. I saw there were two unopened parchments. I wondered if they should be read in case there was something important.'

Quentus finished sopping up the last of the hommus.

'The master left everything for me to place in the chest. He would have seen the scrolls and opened them if he thought they were important.'

Jenna looked at Quentus. He doesn't understand.

'I noticed one of them……'

'I think it is time for me to show you where to sleep so you can rest. The journey north is long and a storm may delay you if you are unlucky. Although I somehow think that the desert will look very kindly upon you Jenna. After all even the ocean was unable to stop you and the desert no longer has the sun to rely upon to tame man's desire to seek out other places. The wind is its only friend.'

Jenna followed Quentus to a small room at the side of the kitchen area. It had a stone bed with a reed mattress. It would be warm against the night air.

She turned to thank Quentus but he had already gone.

She did not sleep due to the hardness of the bed against her aching ribs. Upon seeing the dawn meander through the small slit that passed for a window she decided it was time to leave. She walked out to the courtyard. She poured some water from the pitcher on the table. Eating a fig she went to find the servant. She found him still asleep on the floor of the kitchen. She thought of the cushions in the master's room and the comfort they would bring for a short while at least.

As she turned to leave her foot trod on a twig and the snapping rebounded in the silence of the courtyard. The servant woke jumping to his feet.

'Did you rest well?'

'I did.' She decided there was no point in saying anything other than that.

'I will fetch you some food for the journey.'

'I only ask for some of the bread.'

She walked out and saw Augustus lounging under a palm tree. It was a beautiful place and the castle looked majestically austere in its solitary rule of the sands.

She rubbed Augustus on the nose. He burped at her.

'You will need to follow the large dune we crossed all the way until the mountains of Egypt are seen. If you keep to the ridge it will lead you directly there.'

'I will follow them until the cliffs of Madrid are seen. I will need to swim again.'

'I only know until the coast of Egypt. I do not know if the ocean is still there but again to cross the angry seas from Singapore makes you the ocean's master and not the other way around.'

'Quentus, I want to tell you something before I go. Please understand I am doing this not to make you feel less then what you are but in the hope that it may bring you some freedom or enliven a desire that may now be fulfilled when once it thought impossible. Do you understand me? Sometimes we do things because we have to and sometimes because it simply fills in time.'

'I think so. You wish me to have a choice that I once would never have considered.'

'Yes that's it exactly.' Jenna took a breath, relieved that the servant understood her intention.

'One of the scrolls was marked with the black seal of the Bondmasters when one of their kind has forfeited their rule.'

'Yes I have seen this.'

'Do you understand what that means? Your master has left his jurisdiction and unless there was a very good reason for it he would have been hunted down and executed. Or even if he did outrun the Purgers, he will not be coming back. I don't understand why he chose not to tell you this. I am truly sorry if he meant to be cruel and keep you chained to a vain and inglorious task when you could have been set free.'

'I believe you Jenna. But I also think the Sheik intended this oasis to be the first place of freedom for himself and those akin to his cause. He was as enslaved as me and sought to change things. A castle built of sand from the toil of honest hands to witness all that can pass until it or me dies. It was a noble dream I believe; a noble cause for me to be chained to. I will not leave.'

Jenna smiled realising that Quentus understood more than she did.

'Aha I have been arrogant in my musing Quentus. I assume too much.'

'If my turrets cast the last shadow when the final winter comes then I will die happy and fulfilled in my purpose. What more can I ask for as a slave?'

'I am truly grateful for your hospitality Quentus.'

'I think you will make it to your home Jenna.'

Jenna walked into the desert away from the oasis. As it blurred into a mirage and finally disappeared she thought I wish there was enough time to see Quentus' castle fully built and the last paintings on Jack's windows.

5 Letter Six

I am still in old China, at the base of the mountains. It has been many winters here and I feel this would be as close to a home besides you which I have ever felt. The people seem kind for the most part but their lives are short as the plagues become more ferocious. This shortness of existence leads to both humility and acts of kindness but much opportunism against the weaker ones.

I am considered strong because the sickness doesn't take me. My hair loses its colour and becomes grey like the granite that makes the mountains. They think I am full of wisdom and knowledge because of this. I have been able to teach the children here even though most of them don't survive to have their own. I asked one of the elders what was the purpose of learning if we all would die anyway.

He replied 'Nothing can stop humans standing and looking upon the horizon and seeking the possibilities that lie beyond it. Once the sun dies then there will be nothing more to see or ponder. But for one hundred years I have been waiting for that moment when everything ceases to exist. So at what time in my life was I allowed to lie down and no longer peer beyond the edge of my sight? We question and learn all the time whether we like it or not. And even if we choose to only look at the ground, our mind and hearts will doubt themselves that it is truly stone beneath our feet. So we will continue to search for the answers to the questions we invent. For those who lay dominion over the hearts and minds of others, they will always fail to maintain their leash on power. It is the sun in the sky that will decide when we will no longer desire and our minds no longer question. It is not our fate to make that decision.'

For a moment I thought I heard you in that old man's words. You spoke to me once of people called ancient philosophers; one of them in particular from your lands who spoke of doubt being the way to truth so as to avoid deception. We no longer doubt that the sun will die and have stopped our quest for truth and live in a world bled dry of any desire for the unknown. We merely survive from day to day so we can meet our needs. Was it my doubt that Paris and its artists of antiquity were real that drove me there in the first place? Was it doubt that all those stories about the love that can consume a heart which made me stay with you? Is it the doubt that I may never return that drives me back? Or should I accept that even though our time has not yet come, it will none the less and let go of this foolish longing?

I remember drinking from an old fountain outside a collapsed palace of an ancient King. He was called the Sun King. We had been making our way back from the reckoning, when it was decided that all interlopers should leave. I remember thinking I wonder if he knew how to stop the sun from dying so that I may live my days out with you by my side.

I am coming dear heart

On the horizon she saw the mountains of Egypt. She remembered the path across them that she walked so many years ago. As the sun rose higher and the blurred mirage of the mountains shimmered in the middle of the day she saw something come into her line of vision. Nearing it she saw it was a cross of iron. From it hung a skeleton macerated by the sands. There was nothing to indicate who the person was hanging on the metal coffin. In the centre where the two beams met was a metal arrow embedded securely. The force needed to impale the metal on metal was only known by those hunted down by the Purgers. Such force that it would have lifted the body into position onto the cross beam. Jenna saw a medallion hanging on the arrow. She jumped and managed to pull it off.

Forfeiter was all it said. She guessed it was probably Quentus' master.

She hung the medallion back on to the shaft. As she did so the bone around the chest disintegrated causing a chain reaction. The skeleton crumbled into the sand and almost disappeared.

Jenna pushed sand over the skull as a casual act of burial for the Sheik.

'I hope you finish your castle Quentus and enjoy the reward of your labour. Your master will not lay eyes upon it nor have reason to beat you again.'

The great dune she had been following began to curve towards the west and downwards. It was a long trek from memory. It had been the loneliest part of that journey so long ago. After fleeing the Great Purge she had struggled onto the rocks of the cliffs of Europa like a piece of detritus; forced away from what was a meagre existence at best but seemed to threaten the masters the most; the soil of Africa offering a faint scent of a new life to wash away the pain of the old one.

Her lips were cracked. She checked the cask Quentus had given her. It was half empty. Each step seemed to magnify the crunching of sand grains giving way under her weight. Her eyes scanned looking for the long deep shadow that she remembered the figure had cast once before. Then her mind turned to the image of the skeleton on the cross. How would the Bondmasters know of the Sheik's designs and his attempt to flee? They knew everything because deception was a waste of time. They knew because in the beginning after the wars of attrition everyone was made in the factories. The Purgers retained the memory of every Bondmaster's code.

As each foot dug into the sand and dragged itself out she began to think of Quentus; she thought of him placing every brick and stone into place, the precision of his chisel shaping the hewn rock to fit in exactly. The mortar laid on like thick cake icing and his trowel delicately gluing the walls together in a neat finish. The daydream blurred into her grandmother's arthritic fingers as she remembered her icing a birthday cake for Jack.

The spatula moved slowly over the baked dough; white with brown swirls. It looked so extravagant and rich. Jenna's mouth watered like it did at that time. As she bit into it there was a vague hint of vegetables. Somehow her grandmother had whipped the potato into a creamy paste.

'I used some of the milk tea to make it smoother and to resemble chocolate' was all the old woman had said.

The dough underneath was dry but sweetened with pumpkin flesh.

'I want to learn how to do this.' Jenna had resolutely decided at that moment 'Cakes are delicious to look at Grandmother. How much better they must have been when they had taste. Do you remember the taste of a real cake?'

'I do. I was only 5 years old at the time. It was my birthday as well. It had pink icing with red lollies to make rosebuds. Inside was white sponge layered with five layers of cream and raspberry jam. Oh it was the most beautiful thing I had ever seen and tasted.'

Jenna had noticed a tear fall down her grandmother's cheek.

'My mother came out with the candles twinkling brightly. Five little sparks of light for my age.'

'It must be sadder to know these things and see them gone then to never know them.' spoke Jenna.

'Yes it is Jen. It truly is. Whoever spoke the phrase ignorance is bliss, tis folly to be wise understood the sorrow knowledge brings.'

The creation of things into other things has lessened but not stopped. It all lies within our hearts now instead of in the world. The Purgers could erase any dream made real in a moment now Grandmother. You knew old woman what was to come. Jenna sighed. A sudden gust of wind spat sand in her face rousing her out of her daydreaming. She took her shawl and wrapped it around her head as protection. The mild whistle of the wind soon grew to a raging sand storm.

She saw the slip face of a large dune and decided that was a good place to wait the storm out. The wind roared around her in a deafening force. She dug a small space and breathed the gritty air in between the miniscule grains.

'Soon, soon be patient slave.' She whispered to herself. The weight of the sand increased steadily. It pressed on her chest and stomach. The ribs that were bruised began to ache from the pressure. Jenna waited for it to burn itself out as she knew it would. The memory of crossing these lands before came back to her. A storm had come to her at that time as well and she knew the wind had neither the tenacity nor menace of the ocean. There had been so many things to endure in her life this was the least of them. A gnawing doubt filled her mind as the sand filled every crevice made by her limbs and body. Why was she doing this?

'Soon, soon, be patient slave.' The words repeated themselves but how meaningless they were. She had been no more a slave than the sand or ocean. She had been as tempestuous and head strong as both of them. No bonds had lay around her feet or leash around her neck. Everything that had happened had been her choice to make. And they had been choices. At no time had anyone held a knife to her throat or made her state her cause or swear a vow against those she held most dear.

'What a foolish princess you are Jenna Louise Tenebrae.'

The gloom of twilight slowly made its way across the dunes and over the buried form of Jenna. With it the scream of the abrading wind worked itself to one further crescendo and then suddenly died to a soft whisper. Jenna dug herself out and climbed to the top of the mountain of sand that had grown around her. She searched for the land mark that would signal where she needed to walk to make it to the sea of Europa. For an age the lonely figure stood watching but could not find what she was searching for.

She swallowed feeling the sand grains scrape against her throat and moved forward. There was no choice now. The mountains stood to her left and that would have to serve as her compass. Everything in her sight was smothered when once there were old roads and ancient obelisks and pyramids that had withstood all the ages of her kind. And there used to be a river as well; a mighty river that fed the people and land alike. Now the sand had taken back what it gave away so many millennia ago.

'I wonder if Quentus had ever seen those monuments built by the bonded just like him.'

Her feet dug into the softness but instead of comfort came pain as her old legs strained harder to walk. Soon she began to sink ankle deep then half way up her shins. Stopping on the crest of a large dune regaining her breath she sipped some water and felt a momentary relief. Her eyes scanned and then stopped. There it was. The place she had been looking for.

The shadow of the creature's head stretched out to her almost as if it wanted to clutch her living flesh as if it were its own. The rest of the face lay buried under the sand leaving only the trapezoid shape of the head. One eye watched implacably, unblinking as the tiny figure of Jenna approached.

'I saw you in all your splendour once long ago and now the desert that made you has taken you back into its bosom.'

She stood on top of the great Sphinx feeling as if she had conquered the desert and all that had come before. Even this great watcher of the ages of men and lands now lay suffocating in the womb of its creation. But Jenna had survived all of this to stand upon the crown of this ancient monument and see her path far away to the north. She breathed in the dry air and let it sting her throat and chest.

'I am coming dear heart.' She called into the emptiness around her and willed the echo of her voice to Gabriel.

She sat down and drank some water. The mountains stood behind her and she would need to walk straight ahead for many miles until she found the sea. It neared evermore. The small doubt that all was in vain came to her, but she pushed it aside quickly.

She took a piece of chipped rock and began to carve her name into the eye of the Sphinx.

'Watch me until you no longer can and then remember me. My life mattered no more than the slaves that built you long ago, but you are still here as the memory of their lives and so you shall be for mine.'

She climbed back to the dunes. Her feet and legs cried for the hardness of the shaped rock as they sunk once again into the soft grains. Each step weighed a thousand tonnes as the horizon never seemed to get any closer. She looked back and the small hump of the Sphinx was just discernible.

'Keep watching, the slave makes its escape.'

Jenna turned her thoughts away from the desert to Gabriel. He had been reading to her. They had stolen away to the cellar after working all day and night clearing rubble from a building that had been demolished. He had un-wrapped a leather pouch and pulled out a tablet that still worked. She was amazed after all this time. She remembered fingering the screen to see if it was real. He was reading a story called Les Miserables. The only section that remained legible was about a character called Fantine. The passage was describing her dying. Jenna had begun to cry.

'Why do you cry for them and not for us?' asked Gabriel stopping all of a sudden.

'I don't know. I guess our lives are just as bleak but the words draw out more from my heart then anything I have felt or seen.'

'But at least these people had their chance to live in ignorance until death takes them. We sit and wait for it. I would prefer not to know. I prefer the purity of their innocence. Ours has been lost to the shadow of certainty.' replied Gabriel.

'I guess so. I hadn't thought of that. No I think it is right to weep for Fantine. She only knew of misery but lived in hope of a better day or redemption. We have none. How can we be sorrowful and weep when we have seen what now meets us in the end? I grieve for their naïve hope that was so real to their hearts.'

Gabriel smiled at her comment and continued to read.

She felt water lap over her feet. It roused her instantly. In front of her the desert bled into a vast azure ocean. The blue was so indelible that even the ruminant grey sky brightened. For the first time in her life Jenna looked upon an unblemished oasis of nature. Before her birds pricked the water's mirrored surface looking for fish. Little crabs bobbed up from beneath the sand. Pink flamingos stood elegantly preening themselves. A flock of yellow legged gulls fluttered as a ripple disturbed where they stood on the shore. Their abrading cry cracked the still air. Brindle skimmers arrowed over her head making her duck. A little brown blob of fur shot after the larger bird. The mother fed her baby with its large orange beak spewing a crab into the mouth of the chick.

A dampness suffused into her skin washing away the grains of sand etched into the delicate flesh. Jenna stood on the bay of Northern Africa. Sipping some water from her cask she noticed its staleness intensified by the uncorrupted beauty surrounding her.

Falling to her knees she wept silently. She sat in paradise and nothing not even what waited for her would match it. How had it survived for so long in a world that slowly died? The harmony of perfection could not be interrupted. Its grasp could not be loosened. In trueness to its own rubric, like those humans so long ago, the earth laid its soul bare before her and would not be diminished, not even by the treachery of a dying sun.

'I wish this wasn't happening to the world. I want to keep it alive. This makes me weep Gabriel, just like the words made me weep for Fantine. Great watcher in the desert can't you stop it?' The thought of losing this more than anything else gouged a great hollowness inside her. Within that egregious silence the reality that she ran not just to her beloved but also her impending death and all that had existed to make her, loomed like an eternal abyss. Never before had that truth been so clearly allowed to penetrate her conscious or thoughts.

Across the pristine tableau she could see the cliffs of Europa. It was only a half day swim to the lands of her home, but for the first time in almost sixty seasons Jenna wanted to lie down and witness the last days in this place. As she sat listening to the music of the earth she felt the leather pouch move. Gabriel's voice came to her 'It is our minute desires that matter. The world will not care what they are so in the end we must.'

'I am coming dear heart for whatever it is worth.'

This time her mantra was soaked in grief rather than hope.

6 Letter Five

I sit on a precipice of a great mountain. I feel giddy at the expansive view before me. There is a large eagle circling. Its mottled grey feathers are contrasted against the rare cerulean blue of a clear sky. The bird must have seen something to eat. I imagine this is what a king would have looked like regally surveying his realm. Such elegance can only be matched by the mountain itself and even then it is vanquished by the bird's command of the air. It spears down to a cliff ledge. Its talons clasp a rodent. It darts away in one liquid movement. There is no interruption to the rhythm and law that allows this spectacle. There is no bond that tethers its desire to sustain its own life or take that of another. Surely this is what a ruler truly is and surely this is what freedom can truly be. Is it a god or king or merely the perfection of the world made visible.

Why is it my mind understands the completeness of all that I see now and yet my heart remains so utterly unfulfilled? Is it a punishment? How can this majestic beast ask for nothing and yet it is given everything, while we below sit here with empty hearts and bellies?

I envy this great creature. You and I will never know such freedom or its kinship with the world. Forever we are condemned to be strangers in this cradle and never released from its confines.

Perhaps this is why the sun chooses to die, to mock us. For if our inexhaustible fountain of hopes and desires were ever set free, I believe they would drown the sun and its ascendency over us.

I have travelled far into the southern lands of Old China. There are more people but they die young. They think it is strange to see someone like me; plump with dirty golden hair. I am taking the reed cloth that was spun in the islands to sell here. It is easy work to barter the cloth. The people need its warmth to survive the winters.

This place bustles like your home but in a different rhythm. Like you it seems ancient and untouched from the greater world around it. The people's memories are longer.

I will stay and learn of their ways if I am welcome.

I am coming dear heart

'I saw her swimming. She came up over there.'

The black leather clad figures sat upon horses with their cross bows slung across their back.

'Ride to the northern ridge. We will go south and pincer her.'

The hooves thundered down the orange slated road. The Madrid outpost was always manned as it was the last place where a person could easily cross into Europa from the southern territories. Everywhere else the lands had become too hostile to travel. So they knew the ones who made it to this far had tenacity and resources to survive. They could be enslaved or killed if they proved too unwieldy. Forfeiters were instantly reclaimed or killed if their codes were too degenerated.

Jenna slept under a tree. Her clothes had dried from the swim as the day had warmed. Ants crawled on her toes, and flies buzzed near her face. The olive tree offered fruit which was edible. She had drifted off to sleep wondering how many olives she would be able stuff into her sack.

In her dream she lay with Gabriel. His arms around her and his breathe tickling her neck. The serenity seemed unbreakable. In the peace of her sleep came the thundering boom again. An image of the blue door of his place exploding suddenly appeared in her dream. The sound woke her but when she blinked all she saw was dust that had been disturbed from the road. She realised horses had just ridden past. She scrunched herself behind the slab of rock that had hidden her from the riders. She waited, her chest heaving. Her eyes darted left and right trying to see a path that lead away from the road. She ducked again as the sound of more hooves neared. She swallowed.

'Where slave, where can you hide?' she whispered

Her path to the mountains was behind her but the Purgers would be able to see her from the road. On the other side lay a steep cliff that only led down to the ocean. She had gouged her shins and torn her nails climbing up the jagged rocks.

The olive tree was the only place to find food for many miles. They would guess she was here.

She got up and darted across to the cliff and indelicately scrambled under an overhanging ledge. She hid in a crevice made by a rock that had cracked in two. The hooves neared again but instead of flying past they slowed in their pace until she heard a slow trot.

'She has to be here somewhere. Ya can't get far enough from sight in one day. Yeah look this grass has been flattened. She'll be here somewhere.'

Then she heard them dismount. She squeezed in tighter against the red sandstone. She cursed herself and her body. She had tired so much from the swim that she had been forced to come ashore. It had been too close to the outpost and they had seen her. She had forgotten in her fatigued stupor that they would be keeping a look out. It didn't bode well after all these years they still patrolled the southern border so strictly. She had thought that it may have waned as fewer people lived or were allowed to travel beyond their encoded territories. But no, the leash was still held with a deathless grip.

Suddenly a hand and then leg came over the edge. Her heart thudded. This is the end. She had come this far after so many years to be captured like a trapped hare.

The cross bow glinted just slightly in the sun. It was ornately decorated and polished. He was an experienced patroller. They were rewarded with more sturdy weapons if they made a certain score of captures. How many were there? The horses had sounded like a troop. She had heard only one voice but it spoke to another.

'See anything?'

That was the second one.

'No…' suddenly their eyes met.

Purgers all looked the same as they were descended from the one genetic line. They were remnants of the armies that had fought in the fourth war of attrition. The strongest warriors who had survived from the great battles were rounded up. Successive generations of breeding produced the Purgers along with the Bondmasters.

The small mouth sneered revealing the pointy yellow teeth as the soldier saw Jenna crouched in the dark crevice. He slowly reached for his crossbow. She gripped a loose rock. She had to try and risk it. She was dead either way. She pegged it with lightning speed at him. It hit him on the forehead. She saw it unbalance him enough. She flung herself at him. He grabbed her and wrenched her onto a jagged boulder. It winded her badly. Gasping she pulled away but not without grabbing a metal arrow from his belt. She kicked at him. He stumbled backwards and fell. She slid up under the ledge again. She dug the arrow into the hand of the next soldier above her as he watched. She slashed until the man grunted deeply pulling away. The other one came scrambling towards her from below. She stood up hoping the other was wounded enough not to be able to use his bow. She rushed at the one approaching her. She lunged at him hoping to force him down the cliff face. As she landed on top of him his footing slipped on the mossy stones and they careened down the slope. She heard his back crack. He went limp.

She swung back and saw the other one fumbling with his weapon. There were only two. She grabbed another rock. For a second she imagined she was playing charlie with Jack and Kat and pegged it at him. It struck the soldier on his face but didn't knock him out.

She ran towards the path. The metal arrow sparkled on the sandstone. She picked it up. The Purger nearly had his bow mounted. She scrambled over the edge her old body weak and not willing to give anymore strength. She heard the snick of the cross bow as it fired. She ducked. The arrow speared the dirt near her feet. She launched again and fell onto the Purger. A horse reared up behind her. He stumbled but was too strong for her to push over. She dug the arrow as hard as could into his arm. It barely pierced the thick leather. Feeling it a give a little she drove it in harder. He grunted and wrenched her up by her hair. A blade came near her face. His eyes were like a spider; black and unreadable. She looked at him and wondered what his name was. It was doubtful that he knew himself.

She put her hands up and tried to gouge those eyes out .The blade began to slip deeper into her skin. Blood trickled down her throat. She pulled back suddenly. His hand slipped as the blood oozed under his glove. She fell back onto the gravel. She felt an arrow under her hand and picked it up. The Purger readied his cross bow above her. His view too clear and aim too accurate for her to flee fast enough and survive. Getting up with the arrow in her hand she walked towards him. He waited for her.

'I will wait until you are in front of the tree and then I will pin your carcass to it.' The voice was thick and flat. They had no accent, no history and no name. Bred purely to hunt, they no longer recognised their own kind.

Jenna moved quickly and threw herself at him with enough strength to smother the crossbow. The snick of the arrow was barely audible. She felt the force of the weapon pierce her shoulder. She jabbed the arrow into his face ferociously and unrelenting. It was now or never. He stumbled. She kept stabbing until the tip of the arrow stuck. Suddenly the resistance put up by the hunter slackened. The two of them pulled away. The arrow lay embedded in his eye.

He held up the crossbow but seizing the moment she ran at him again; the arrow in his head grazing her face. She wrestled for the weapon in his hand. His grip was impossible to break. She found a rock. One of his hands latched around her throat. She hammered the stone down onto the arrow and pushed it in further. He went limp under her just as she blacked out from his hand choking her.

She got off the Purger and threw up. She looked at the body. How long before more came? She looked at the horses. There was no point trying to ride one of them. They will always go back to their stations. They both stood silent and still like black obsidian statues. Are you even flesh and blood she wondered? She took their reins and tied them to the olive tree.

Blood poured from the wound in her shoulder. It throbbed terribly but she didn't want to remove the arrow yet. It would help keep the torn flesh sealed. She ripped the bottom of her tunic and placed it over the wound and then took another strip and tightened it like a tourniquet. She tested her arm and could move it with pain.

She began to tear off branches from the olive tree and removed the fruit for her satchel. She filled it easily. She slung it over her shoulder. The leather pouch slid under her tunic. It was dry and safe. She took the cross bow and slung it on her back. She could only find two arrows. She placed them in her satchel.

Looking at the body on the ground made her feel sick again. Does this act obliterate all other acts of kindness Grandmother?

She walked up over the ridge. She looked across the plateau that reached all the way to the northern mountains; they had been called the Pyrenees once. The town had been nestled in the ridge half way up the first face. It did not lessen her fear as the great open plains lay before her. She could be seen from every direction. There was no escaping if they came for her. It was only a day's march to the mountain village but with nowhere to hide if they pursued her it would be her death march.

'Just go Jenna, there is no other way.'

She had no strength left to run so she began to walk.

The face of the dead Purger kept invading her mind but she pushed it back. There had been no choice.

The day darkened soon enough. She noticed for the first time the indigo hue of the dusk. Normally it went from dull grey to black over a long drawn out sunset. Occasionally a flare of vermillion would pervade the morbidity of the twilight but not on this day. A sense of doom suddenly overwhelmed her as the dark came. She sobbed in the emptiness so sure of the feeling that she would not make it back to him.

'Soon, soon be patient slave.' She whispered to herself.

The night was completely silent as she walked. She listened keenly for any sound of hooves beating a path behind her but so far she heard nothing. Why she wondered?

She kept going looking intently at the tiny glow of lights from the little village. They often disappeared but then would come back into her vision like a sign post to keep in her in the right direction. Close to the dawn her legs buckled from exhaustion. She rested propped against a rock and watched the lands behind her. It was so still and empty. It was not comforting like it had been in the desert. The barren plains seemed to reflect her own fear like a clean flat altar waiting for the spill of the sacrifice.

She spat the pips out of the green olives and then sipped some water. She half dozed until the pale disc broke the mountain ridge and pierced the dirt where she walked. As she stood, tears welled in her eyes from the pain in her shoulder and the cramps in her legs.

'Keep going this last little bit.' She wheezed 'Watcher in the desert, keep watching the runaway slave. Trees in the mountains hide the slave when she arrives.'

She limped until her muscles loosened. It was slow and her mind drifted again. She and Gabriel were digging to build a wall to keep people out and those inside as prisoners. He had taken her hand and led her to the part of the wall they had just finished.

'This is for you and me.'

Looking down where the mangled construction of the wall met the ground, she saw the figure of the statue of winter. He had mortared the old woman into a large slab of stone. Gabriel placed his hand on the head and pulled the brick free.

'A way out or a way in.' She had remembered thinking it was like the statue had now become a gatekeeper between the old world that had watched the horizon and the one that now sat behind walls waiting for death with no way out.

The beating rhythm of the hooves aroused her. She turned and saw them coming across the plains. She was only a few miles from being able to hide in the forests at the base of the mountains. She tried to start running but her legs would not move any quicker.

'Keep walking as far as you can.' She pulled the crossbow off her back and loaded it. She turned and saw them, they were still tiny specs but the metallic horseshoes echoed strongly in the emptiness. She saw there were only two. The trees neared as did the Purgers behind her. Her mind became blank not wanting to think about what may happen. She willed her rebellious legs to take each step towards the safety of the trees.

The first arrow flew past as a branch of a great pine brushed her face. She ran into the forest blindly as the pale light of the dawn darkened instantly from the density of the branches.

At least they will need to get off their horses she thought. She walked in as far as she could and stood still behind a trunk. She heard the crunch of the footsteps. They would find her. She gripped the cross bow. I can only attack one and the other will come and kill me.

Suddenly one of them appeared before her. Startled she shot off the weapon into his face. It hit. Thinking quickly she grabbed him and leaned him up against the tree to stop the noise of his body hitting the ground. She shuddered at the unnatural lightness of the hunter.

She saw a trail that lead to the road to the village. She darted towards it. The other one had not found her yet. She was still covered by the bushes and began to make good progress. She didn't look down the slope but directly above her at the flat road. If he got her he got her.

'Keep going slave.' She hissed to herself.

The arrow shot past grazing her ear. Her hand touched the smooth surface of the worn road and gripped. She hoisted herself over. He would be here in seconds. But she had the high ground she thought. The Purger scurried over the rubble and stone at an unnatural manic pace; the implanted arachnid DNA perfectly reproduced in his movements. She loaded the cross bow. She aimed. She fired it and it hit him. Only in the shoulder but it wounded one of his arms. The climb was too steep to cling to the rocks with one. It would slow him down.

Jenna fled towards the village. It was only a mile away. She could see smoke rising. She limped as fast as she could; each step felt like she was moving through mud. The cross bow lay in her hand. All the arrows had gone. She could only use it as a club if he caught her. The first huts began to appear along the side of the road. It was nearing midday but no one was out. She searched for the house. It still had to be here. She saw it as she rounded a bend which revealed the whole village. There at the end sat the white hut. It had not changed except the thatch needed repairing. It did not rain much here so there would be no great hurry to fix it.

Then her heart sank. She heard the hooves thundering behind her. But how?

She turned and saw a group of Purgers coming along the road. They weren't the same ones but they would ask questions. She darted into the closest hut. Inside was dark. A candle sat burning in a lamp on a table. It seemed empty. She peered out of the window. The horses streaked past like a black lightening rod.

'Who is there?'

Jenna started slightly at the voice.

'I am sorry. I will leave in a moment. I didn't want to be detained by the Purgers.'

'Those bastids. On the hunt all the time. I heard there have been riots at the great ships.'

'I must go I am sorry.'

She looked out to the road and couldn't see anything. Taking the chance she raced towards the white cottage.

Three houses away she looked back and her heart froze. Coming along the road was the one who hunted her but worst still there were more galloping behind. She steered towards the cottage. But he would see which one she went into. She had no choice. She kept going hoping it would provide some refuge. She reached the brown wooden door and knocked frantically. She stared along the path and watched as the group of hunters gained on their wounded comrade and then in astonishment she saw them ride over the top of him. His body rolled underneath; limbs flailing as they were shattered into a thousand pieces. She rapped again panic overwhelming her as the black miasma of killers came closer.

Someone opened the door just as the Purgers sped past. She turned and saw a young woman standing in front of her. They both startled one another. Jenna hadn't expected to see someone else here.

'What do you want? It is dangerous out there.' The girl's eyes darted behind Jenna.

'They have gone.'

'No there will be more. What do you want? Who are you?'

'I am looking for Katlin Tenebrae. I am her sister Jenna.'

7 Letter Four

Music fills the air tonight. It comes from the stalks of the water lilies which grow along the shoreline. The bonded chisel holes out of them, turning them into instruments of music. As we wait to be taken to the mainland the lilting melodies float into the night towards the stars. The sounds are restful and peaceful and gently cradle us in its soothing notes. I left the island long ago by a boat that I stowed away on. It took me to the hot lands that lie further east and left me marooned on the highest tip of Van Diemen's Isle. The sun beats relentlessly and drains all my strength. Then the rains begin and they beat relentlessly as well. So different to where you are. My feet cry for the firmness of ancient roads of the Romans and the touch of man's hand in all things. In this place nature is unsparing as it knows it remains master over all.

My days are spent gathering branches and fallen leaves from the palms and ferns to make cloth. It is coarse but once it is boiled and spun it is bearable against the skin. It seems this work calms me for I have not wept for a long time and while my heart still aches for the sight of you, it now lets the memories of you wash over it and enjoy the happiness they bring.

I was climbing a hill one morning; the red dawn was spectacular in its threat of the heat it would birth. It reminded of a time when we decided to have a meal called a picnic. We climbed the old ruins to the very top as the sun rose. It was in a place full of tombstones and legends. The names had been mostly worn off but you seemed to know who lay in those graves. I remember some of the names which remained Chopin, Morrison and another Wilde; you lingered over this one the longest. You said they were ancient poets. I remember the one you called Wilde. You recited his poem The Artist to me. It is the last line that is etched in my heart 'And out of the bronze of the image of The Sorrow that endureth for Ever he fashioned an image of The Pleasure that abideth for a Moment.'

My grandmother often read poetry to us as children. I did not understand its purpose. It seems to me if you have something to say then simply write it and let the words speak. But it called to me nonetheless in its vagueness and encrypted meanings. It was like it spoke the language of the heart. Or is that how I learnt that there was a language of the heart not just the rationale which the mind allows or the savage machinations of the Bondmasters and Purgers?

The pipers stop their playing as the boats draw near. The people clamber aboard willingly. I wonder what those poets who surrounded us as we picnicked sounded like. I wonder what they thought of the world around them. What did they see beyond the horizon?

My heart is at rest today. It beats full of the memories of you and the poetry of a water lily's brittle stem as it is caressed by the breath of a slave.

I am coming dear heart.

'Jenna.'

Kat lay on the bed. Jenna took her sister's hands. They felt like the dry compressed tree she used to write her letters.

'How can you be alive? Most slaves die before their masters.' croaked Kat

'Nice to see you as well sister' she replied sardonically.

'Hmph' Kat tried to laugh at the rebuff but it made her go into a coughing fit instead.

'What is wrong with you?'

'Smoking.'

'We look old.'

'We are old.'

'I saw Jack.'

'Where?'

'Coast above Singapore Bay.'

'He said he always wanted to go there.'

'Did he?'

'We all had a choice at the beginning but that changed for the new comers.'

'Like me.'

Jenna's sister smiled as she whispered 'Yes like you Jen.'

Jenna watched the old woman before her begin to doze. Her memories of Kat were few as a child. She remembered more of Jack and their grandmother. Kat had helped her once and she had wanted to thank her. At least she would have this chance.

'Kerilyn will make you some food. I want to sleep.'

She let go of Jenna's hand.

'I just wanted to say…'

The eyes roused and looked directly at Jenna with the same daring haughtiness that had irritated her as a girl.

'I'm not intending to drop dead yet.'

Jenna smiled and got up.

Her shoulder ached dully but was comfortable with the sling and ointment Kerilyn had put on the wound. The tip of the arrow came out more easily then she had expected. Jenna guessed that Kerilyn had fixed these sorts of wounds many times for her slaves.

Walking out of the bedroom she entered a main hall that led to the kitchen area. A familiar smell met her but she couldn't remember what it was. The young woman stood stirring a large pot in the hearth. The table was set for two places with wooden bowls and spoons on a reed tablecloth.

'Sit.'

The girl kept her back to Jenna as she sat at the table. She traced the familiar shape of her family in the girl's figure.

'I can serve myself.'

'No it is easier for me to bring it to you.' She turned and walked to the table and took a bowl.

'Thank you Kerilyn.'

'Is Grandmother asleep?' she bought the full bowl over to Jenna and took the other one.

'She is.'

Before coming to sit down she hesitated as the sound of thunder shuddered through the house.

'More of them. So many now.' spoke Kerilyn 'I have never seen so many.'

Jenna felt dread crawl over her as the memory of their pursuit invaded her mind. Kerilyn sat down and began to eat.

'Is there something wrong?'

Jenna realised she had been staring.

'Oh no. I'm sorry. I can see Kat in you as a young woman that is all. I never knew your mother.'

'Neither did I. She died at child birth.'

Jenna nodded; another lost link in the Tenebrae chain like her own parents. She hadn't known them either.

'It must be a long time since you last saw my grandmother then.'

'It was before your mother was born.'

Kerilyn nodded.

Jenna didn't elaborate on her last meeting with Kat. It had been a desperate race across the lands when she had fled the Purgers to remain un-bonded. Her sister had given her refuge back then as she did now.

'Were you all forced apart from one another? Grandmother never spoke of you. She occasionally mentioned a brother.'

'Kat left when I was young. We barely knew one another.'

The girl nodded accepting the answer on its face value. In part it was true. Kat had left when Jenna was only a child.

'Where have you been all this time then?'

'I have been bonded in the southern islands of Asia. I have been freed and wanted to see Kat before it is too late. This stew, I have tasted it before.'

'Grandmother said her grandmother had taught her to make it. She said it is not the same though as the herbs for it will no longer grow in the dirt here.'

Jenna nodded realizing it was the tarragon stew they would have as a special treat when meat could be found. Sorrow welled in her heart as she remembered her and Kat and Grandmother each taking turns to stir the thick liquid as it marinated on the fire.

'I think I will rest a while.'

'Grandmother will sleep the rest of the day. It would have exhausted her to see…..

She stopped speaking before finishing the sentence.

'I understand.'

'Why didn't Grandmother speak about you?' Jenna noticed the piercing gaze and for a brief moment saw her own grandmother looking at her. She shivered as she did not feel love and compassion but the frigid chill of a winter's dark heart.

'We were not friends. We were different. Ask your grandmother what I was like as a child. She knows how I can be at times.'

Jenna smiled slightly as she avoided the questions. She turned quickly to go to the small pantry room that had been converted to a place for her to sleep. Kerilyn did not speak again as she took the bowls from the table. Jenna laid her swag out. She saw the young woman sit down at a spinning wheel with some white thread. It was corn thread, spun from the silk of the husks. Jenna pulled the curtain across and lay down. The young woman inside was her grandniece but a stranger as well. She would know it was not right that Jenna had come like this to Kat. She would know that families were either the bonded or the masters. To have both in one family made no sense.

The soft purr of the wheel was comforting and she quickly fell asleep. Gabriel was before her. He was wiping tears off her face.

'It is not our time to end yet.'

The Purgers chased her relentlessly and his face and touch faded as the pounding of their metallic hooves smashed the world to pieces.

She woke. It was almost the morning. The shades of indigo were stronger with each dawn. The shafts of light that pierced the small opening in the cupboard spread a warm glow of violet over everything. Jenna eased herself up against a shelf. Her shoulder screamed at her. As she waited for the pain to ebb she passed her hand through the indigo light. A tear spilled down her cheek as she wondered how the death of the world could bring such beauty.

She heard Kat coughing. Soft murmurs followed as she heard Kerilyn speaking to her grandmother.

Getting up she went to the bedroom. Kat was sitting up. She was wheezing and her face was flushed. Kerilyn was feeding her some of the stew she had made. Jenna nodded at Kat as she went to a chair in the corner of the room.

'Bad night?' she asked.

'Always. Thanks Keri, I have had enough.'

The girl had no expression of worry or concern as she left the room. She seemed to be more like a bonded doing her duty.

'She resents her life and me. She is an honest girl but unloving. I don't blame her. She has too much of my influence in her life. It will be good when I am dead. She will finally become her own person.'

Jenna was surprised at the comment from Kat. She was never one to think that such esoteric matters such as your identity should be indulged in.

'What was her mother like?'

Kat smiled.

'Like you; full of hopes and dreams, things that don't belong to now; different to me.'

'Were you sad when she died?'

'I was actually. You know me too well. Only you would ask that about me.'

'I am glad for you then. Kerilyn knows it is strange that I have come like this.'

'She is honest but will not be loyal if asked. I had our grandmother's influence but that was watered down in her upbringing.'

'I know. I will not stay long.'

'Why did you come back? There will be nothing there for you.'

'I don't believe that.'

Kat shook her head at her little sister. Both old women now but before her sat the heart and mind of the young bride ready to embark on her life.

'The last time I saw you Jenna you were running from the Purgers then. I don't know whether to admire you or pity you, to have survived so long. My own family hunted by the monsters we used to make our every command be obeyed. You listened to our grandmother too well.'

'Perhaps you and Jack didn't listen enough.' Kat smirked at the rebuttal.

'I think it is her that made you capitulate and give me sanctuary all those years ago and still does now Kat.'

Her sister nodded just slightly.

'I am glad at least that I have seen you and Jack again.'

'What happened in the last days of Grandmother's life? The masters would not let me return.'

Jenna was surprised at her question. Kat had often clashed with Grandmother. The memories of the constant admonishments and abrasive tongue of Kat every time Grandmother criticized the masters were what remained engrained in Jenna's mind. If ever a person was born to rule others it was her sister. Jack would have been a kinder Bondmaster than Kat.

'I remember the suffering she went through. She denied herself the privileges that she could have had at the end.'

'She was a stubborn old thing. Like you. I regret not seeing her but it couldn't be helped. It's too long ago now anyway. Did Jack go back?'

'No. Neither of you did.'

Jenna pushed back the tears in her eyes. Kat was the wrong person to show how deep the sorrow lay in relation to their grandmother.

'You shouldn't have stayed Jen. She would not have minded.'

Jenna bristled inwardly at the callous comment.

'You understand nothing.' She replied stonily. She saw Kat's eyes focus on her for a moment at the intended barb.

'Are the roads north clear?'

'As far as I know. The ships are ready and Purgers are being sent to stop them being raided.'

'Don't the Bondmasters know that it will be futile? Nothing will exist after the sun dies.'

'I don't know. It has been planned for a long time. That is why the wars of attrition took place and the rulers agreed to the charter. They wanted to start planning their escape.'

'Is that why forfeiters are hunted down and killed?'

'The ones not useful to them. The more educable ones were placed into the labour camps to design and build the ships or their DNA reclaimed for storage.'

'And the Purgers? Their purpose?'

'Isn't it obvious? They are the ones planning to escape. They know those of us formulated humans that have been endowed with genes for engineering and science. They reclaim our codes for re-population.'

Jenna's mind reeled at Kat's revelation. So the Purgers have become the masters and now seek their escape.

'But it is still futile. In the end what does it matter if the life they are preserving is as bland as parchment to taste.'

'That's what Grandmother used to say. Everything that had made her had been destroyed.' answered Kat.

'How do you think she knew it would mean the end of all things?'

'How do you know she did?'

Jenna looked at Kat intensely. Then her face broke into a smile.

'You haven't changed. It is foolish. Even if things don't die completely, life has been depleted and worn down to whispers and sighs.'

'Why can you pursue your dream and they cannot?'

'Because I do not stop them from pursuing theirs but they will kill me for chasing mine.'

'I wonder how innocent you really are Jenna Louise? I am a Bondmaster and I know what it takes to rule and how bloody my hands are because of it.'

Jenna nodded without answering; the stab of truth as always when uttered from Kat's mouth was lethal in its accuracy.

'Which way will you go?'

'I intend to follow the old Roman road. It is the quickest and there were few settlements along it from memory.'

'I haven't travelled that way for a long time. You can take some supplies. I would leave at night; fewer questions and no goodbyes.'

'I resented you for so long. I hated how much you wanted to be part of this life and the way it worked.' Jenna surprised herself at her candor.

'I know but you were always more sentimental than me. I make no apology for who I am.'

'It's not sentimentalism. It's instinct for me. To have the heart to make things beautiful for no other reason than beauty can exist. Not everything should be about basic survival. Even the bonded who have known nothing else other than what their masters have told them; I have seen them make poetry from the rotten stems of lilies.'

'How am I any different to you? You have done nothing more than the rest of us. I wept for my daughter just as you weep for your precious Paris. The difference is I accept who I am but you never have; yourself or me and Jack.'

Jenna sat looking out the tiny window up towards the cliffs that stood behind the village. Her mind felt the sting of Kats words. It was true she never accepted herself or the others. But it had been whenever her grandmother spoke of antiquity the words of the poets and writers and creations of the artists had felt like they were speaking to her alone. How could she ignore that? She had tried to ignore it and it had made her cruel and unjust.

'I will leave tomorrow. My shoulder heals quickly.'

'The Purgers have all passed. You shouldn't be hindered any further.'

Her heart beat quickened slightly as the next question formed on her lips.

'Does Paris still exist?'

The wait for the answer seemed like an eternity. She didn't want to know. She wanted to discover it for herself. Like the first time. She wanted to see it from her eyes not the bias of another. Let me have this one thing and I will learn to obey she thought. Why did I ask?

'I don't know. I am tired and need to rest.' rasped Kat.

Jenna nodded. So am I she thought to herself as her heart slowed.

Jenna left the room and went to the front door. The street had a few villagers walking along it. The village held no other memory other than Kat's place. She walked out into the cobbled road.

She knew that this was the last time she would see Kat. No sadness lay in her heart, only hollowness at what should have been but never was. That was what she could not explain to her sister; the emptiness that existed now in life. Just in the way Kat and Kerilyn were more like bonded and master, forced to endure their duties until the end. Her own flesh and blood would betray her at moment's notice if the Purgers asked it of her. Even Kat had maintained her deep seated loyalty to her family. But now everything was black and white because there was no time left to see what subtleties could be discovered. It all seemed like a façade waiting to crash down as each ray of the sun poked a hole through its brittle shallowness.

She wandered to the edge of the village and looked down to see the locals tilling crops of capers and artichokes. The tiered layering of the slope spread out below her. It was so uniform and efficient. It was as sculpted as the great pieces of art she had discovered in Paris so many years ago. The inexorable will of humans to bend and shape things to our own ends if only to show what lies in our hearts. That is how we will be remembered if anything remains.

Turning back she heard coughing coming from the house. It was deep and pathological. As she walked in she saw Kerilyn standing over Kat with a bowl. It was full of black spittle.

'It is worse than you said.'

Kat nodded lying back wheezing heavily.

Jenna went to get some water for her sister. Kerylin followed with the black mess and went outside. She tipped the bowl onto the ground and then rinsed it in a bucket.

'She won't last much more. This is the worst I've seen it.'

'What will you do when she dies?' asked Jenna

'Stay here. We are still the Bondmasters.' There was a slight note of offence in her voice.

Jenna didn't know what to do. She wanted to be with Kat but would Kerilyn be trusted to let her go freely. She went back into the bedroom. Kat opened her eyes.

'Please go Jenna. I have only days to live. I feel it. Go to your precious Paris, whatever remains of it.'

You think it is a city I run to she thought. At one time it was Kat but not now.

'I will stay Kat. I am not bound like you and Kerilyn.'

The night came. As her sister lay dying in the bed the indigo of the dusk suffused the air and light. It was peaceful in the little house. Jenna watched Kat's chest move up and down. She wished her peace and was glad that her suffering was not too much. The memory of her grandmother's death was still vivid and haunted her after all these years. Jen had known then what Jack's words meant when he said sometimes the price of bread can be too high. The masters had medicines that could have eased the pain of the septic poison in the old woman but she had refused to accept the privilege. It was on that night she had decided that she must live true to her own heart or all the suffering to be endured would be in vain. Her grandmother's voice floated in her head 'Don't become like them. You have been taught to be better. We are nothing if we are not civilised and discerning in our actions. Only an animal has perfected the art of following their instincts blindly. We have forgotten how to do that well so we must rely on our rational mind to know when to obey and when to use our freedom. Don't become like your brother and sister dear heart. I know that you understand the truth of beauty and the beauty of truth as a poet once wrote.'

Jenna had wept inconsolably when the old woman finally let her last breathe go. Even now she wanted to weep for the loss of her.

'There is stew on the table.' Jenna looked at Kerilyn.

'I don't think she will last the night.'

She didn't speak. Jenna sat at the table and ate. It was blander as it had been watered down to go further but some flavor managed to make its presence known.

'The Purgers will come when she dies to reclaim her codes. You know that.'

'I know.'

'Why did you come here?'

'It was on my way…. I wanted to see her before…' Jenna hesitated as she saw the same predatory expression in Kerilyn's eyes as the Purgers that had hunted her from the coast.

'Give me a day.'

The girl did not reply. Jenna got up and went back to Kat. Her breathing was shallower.

'I will say goodbye now Kat. I wanted to thank you. You saved my life once and gave the petulant bride a chance to pursue her one wish. You did not have to do that. My heart always lay elsewhere to yours but I think underneath, we both understood where it was we should stand in the world.'

She kissed her on the forehead.

Kat's eyes opened and looked at hers briefly 'Go,' she sighed 'She is not me.'

'I know.'

Going into the pantry Jenna gathered her sack. She refilled her water cask and walked straight to the front door. She stopped and looked at Kat in the bed. We are like strangers she thought. I don't even shed a tear for you. I wept more for the stone figures of the fallen palaces and museums of Paris as they were smashed into pieces to build a wall. She opened the door and stepped onto the road.

8 Letter Three

I have been ill. My hair is thinner and my bones almost pierce the skin. The moth eaten moon rose three times before light returned to the island I live on. It is on the coast of Southern Africa. The village where I live was devastated by a plague. Most of the people have died and I was left to lie in a cave. The air would not move through the sludge in my chest making me gasp and wonder if I would ever see you again.

One night I cried for so long because I couldn't remember your face or the sound of your voice. You told me not to worry if our memories faded, as the heart knew to bring us together even when we were still ignorant of one another. You said it knows what it needs before the mind and body and will remember long after fulfillment has passed.

My tears have slowed as the illness finally leaves me. I dreamt last night of the grave where we would meet to rest our exhausted bodies after slaving in the mines. It belonged to the man called Delacroix. The great black slab stood like a rampart of antiquity's beauty. While the fruit for his passion was slowly being torn down by the ruling despots, I believed then that nothing could destroy that unyielding tombstone. It is a memory of humanity's lost beauty and ugliness, a stone writ to give to the dying sun of who we are. Why did we let the ugliness win?

I see young families in the village. The children stare at me but do not speak very much; only their muted sounds of work echo in the silent hills. They cannot read or write. I tried to teach them but one of the father's took my hand away from the wall shaking his head.

It will help them I pleaded. No it will not. Teach them to count so they may barter but nothing more he commanded.

So I write the numbers on the stones and teach them to count. It is such a strange thing that letters no longer have meaning. We don't know how to write what we say. But this was how it began wasn't it? I remember some of the old tablets that showed pictures of where humans came from. Grandmother told me stories of the wars of Origin and the zealotry of those who believed in a creator and those who did not. But when the first black winter blanketed the world the question of our creation was left unanswered as we began to fight for our survival.

The pigeon waits patiently to begin its journey to you with my letter. How does it know to find you?

On my journey here I passed ancient monuments whose grandeur could not be disguised as the desert smudged their edges. I wept when I saw them because for one brief moment I despaired and thought is that all that you and I will become? Will my memories be eroded and turn all that I crave into unheard whispers as the earth seres.

I cannot accept that this is all in vain. Even in my fevered state when despair had me in its clutches trying to convince me that there was nothing more than this life and its constant struggle, I remember that tombstone. I remember the love I bear for you. It will be what drives my flesh to its end.

I am coming dear heart.

She had not seen the sun in all its fullness for many years but when the ash had suddenly cleared she could feel the yellow disc scorching her skin within minutes of the clouds splitting apart. The vision of the great Sphinx lying in the desert came to her. Was this how it had begun? Was this how your sandy tomb started to form around you great Watcher?

Keep watching Watcher, the slave still runs. And as if her whispers echoed through ancient sculpted stones, the marble Roman ruin had come into view heralding her salvation from the incendiary heat. The arch of the stone monument offered shade and she accepted it gladly.

She sat waiting for the twilight so she could begin her journey again. Her mind wandered back to Kat. Her body would have been given over to the Purgers by now and Kerilyn would be the new Bondmaster for the village. Jenna felt no sorrow at her sister's death. The sifted memories were like images on the tablets her grandmother used to show her; pieces of blank parchment waiting for words to give life and feeling.

The road north stretched directly ahead of her. The great ruin where she sat was the centre of a cross roads paved millennia ago. The pale gravel merged with the demure green of an olive grove. The trees looked as old as the road itself; their trunks and branches, contorted from their years on earth. Suddenly the white marble turned cerise. The sun was setting. She wanted to look at it but knew it would blind her in its beauty.

She waited until the cerise bled to indigo and then watched the darkness come. Getting up she could feel the heat of the day pierce her reed sandals as it escaped the ground.

The night was completely silent except for the noise of the gravel crunching under her feet. The sound of it brought the images of the bonded marching from the coast in her mind. They were tied together to prevent them from escaping. She had looked down on the young women from her horse and knew they were her age. The vibrant red of the blood on their feet from the relentless stomping on crushed stone stood out against the dullness of the landscape. They would not have known that in her heart every agonised step and whiplash that struck them, made her want to vomit and run away. But she had not the courage then to follow her own will or to pull the whips from the hands of the Purgers. Even now she was not certain she had the courage to face her life.

'I am not Kat but neither am I like you Grandmother.'

When the day had come with her Charter her grandmother had not spoken to her. She had looked at the old woman and her heart broke.

'I cannot ignore my place. I know what you have taught us is to not give into what the world has become but remember the one that once existed. But I can at least protect a few from its cruelty by being what it asks of me. Come with me Grandmother. I will ask for dispensation under my custody ......'

'How dare you speak like that to me!' the voice had been low and threatening. She had held her breath. She had never seen her grandmother angry until that moment. Her warm brown eyes had flashed at her like a Purger's arrow.

'I will not go with you Jenna. The fact my own flesh and blood offers me slavery should tell you that you should not go either. It will end badly for you. It will make you something that you are not. You are not your sister.'

'I have no choice. I did not choose what my family I was born into.'

'We all have a choice.'

Her grandmother turned on her and went into her room. The curtain falling across the door closing off Jenna's view was like a knife severing all that lay between them. Her protector and sculptor had refused to see her again. Jenna had stood on the verandah of the only home she had known for an hour. The skin on her cheeks had become raw from the tears as they had poured down her face.

'I was weak.' She whispered as she came up over the rise.

In the distance she could see the darker shadow of the great wall of the Keep standing proudly on the mountainside. The road that led towards it was overgrown from the forest which abutted its base. The great birches and oaks all looked tired and grey compared to her last memory of them. The first time she had set eyes upon the trees it had been the last autumn before the long winter. The reds and golds had been magnificent. Her heart had lifted at that moment in her new life as a Bondmaster when the mountainside had presented its fanfare as if in welcome celebration of her arrival.

This time was different, the sorrow and loathing that had dogged her steps seemed fused into the canopy around her. The climb became steeper and the trees denser. The branches above her head wilted with black soot. She touched one of them. It was so brittle that it disintegrated in her hand. She stood still and listened. There was not a sound. No breeze rustled the leaves.

The road became undecipherable as macerated tree roots blocked her path. She stood on one and felt her foot give way. A plume of dust met her in the face and made her cough; the echo jarred the silence. The forest was dead and was waiting for the moment when its bones could melt into the air.

Through the grayness of the forest she saw the ruins of the portcullis. The middle had collapsed leaving each side torn in disunion. She placed her hand on the slab of remaining wall. It was solid and un-giving as it always had been. Often she had stood here greeting the bonded and Purgers feeling the certainty of the stone beneath her hand. She had often asked herself why she could not accept her fate as unfailingly as this castle. It had withstood the stories written in its chambers with no choice so why could she not be the same?

'Who goes there?'

She saw an old man walking down the path towards her. He held a stick in front of him.

She looked at him. His face was familiar.

'Who is it?'

'Friederich, it is me, Jenna.'

He stopped. He looked in her direction but did not seem to see her.

'Master, why have you come back?'

'I came to set you all free.'

'It is not safe. Come inside.'

He turned and she followed. She realised he was almost blind. The path he walked on was a narrow one, worn in a precise way such that the built up ledge acted as a guide.

As she stepped through the elevated doorway a kitchen dominated by a massive hearth yawned at her. The scene instantly drew her back to the first time she had entered the castle. To the right of the great stone mantle was the iron staircase that spiraled towards her old quarters. It was still ornately decorated with intricate carvings of the Knights Brigand; the first masters who built the Keep fifteen centuries ago. Coward criminals who when challenged showed how weak they were but turned into guardians liberated by the people they had oppressed. She had often daydreamed that perhaps the bonded could give this salvation to their masters one day.

Inside the kitchen sat three people. They were as old as her. They were eating.

'The master has returned,' announced Friederich.

All of them looked her way.

'I don't remember your names' was all Jenna could say.

She was so ashamed of her greeting she wanted to disappear into the dead forest unseen.

'It is Robert, Marion and Pierre' replied Friederich.

Jenna sat down near them. They stared at her.

'You are a forfeiter. Why are you here?' asked Pierre

'I came to release you.'

'But you cannot.'

'I can. This land and place is still mine. I came to give writ that your bondage is ended.'

'You were and always will be a fool. What use is our freedom now? I have buried my own children here in this place waiting for release. Where did you go?' spoke Marion

'I left to find my grandmother and then my home.'

'This was your home and we were your bonded.' Pierre's voice was flat and matter of fact.

'I know but it was not my choice to be here.'

'You should have been hunted down by now.' Robert went to the hearth and stirred some stew.

'Have you eaten?'

'No.' He took a bowl and filled it.

'It is not much. The forest is dead now and the soil will no longer give a harvest. Master you may.....'

'Don't call me that Robert. I am no different to you.' She tasted the stew and almost spat it out. It was like eating dirt.

'It was ordained that you would stay and keep this place and us also.'

'It made me cruel to do that Pierre. It tore my heart in two. I took the pain out on you.'

'Like now! Returning to set us free when we are almost dead. I remember you well enough. You are right. You were the cruelest of the masters I knew. Even now you only think of appeasing your own mind. What use is freedom to old bones and limbs that cannot flee to its arms? We would be hunted down for just being alive at our age.'

Robert sat back again. Everyone looked at him astonished at his honesty.

'I cannot change what has happened.'

'We should call the Purgers to have you hoisted to the highest turret.' Marion was stripping branches. Jenna saw the agitation she had caused flow into the violent snapping of the wood as the slave attempted to stoke the weak embers.

'Master your chamber is ready for you.'

Friederich led Jenna up the small spiral staircase. His cane tapped each step as he ascended. The room was laid out exactly the same; a wooden framed bed and green coverlet. A tattered gold curtain floated silently in the window. She had often stood here her heart full of self loathing and longing for her grandmother. Quentus came to mind; the room at the top of his castle; pristine in readiness for its master to return.

'Thank you Friederich.'

She sat on the bed. Mustiness met her.

'You shouldn't have come back.'

'I realise that now but I wanted to try and make it right.'

'You only reopen old wounds.'

'I wanted to close them.'

'Your discontent and cowardice to face your destiny almost killed me when the Purgers would not believe that you had left. The others knew of us being lovers and threw me to their mindless cruelty. They thought I had killed you. I lay bleeding in a pool of blood on the stones of the archway because of you.'

'I am sorry. My grandmother raised us differently and had told me not to come. But I didn't listen. I had visions of being a hero to the bonded in my head, not one of partaking in the cruelty of a world hungry for survival. It was first time I saw a bonded dying; a life scourged out by my hand that made me flee. I was being eaten away as I rent the flesh from the slave's bones. I..I can't even remember the girl's name.' she choked as the memories tore into her mind.

'Did our love mean anything?' he asked as he turned.

Her heart sunk like a stone. How could she tell him it was mere convenience in her darkest moments? Jenna realised what a mistake this had been. Right now they could be signaling the Purgers to come and have her executed. They should despise her.

She was like Adrik; cruel and incompetent. Is this why she had chosen him, to punish herself for leaving her bonded? All I had to do was stay and I couldn't even do that.

'The land here is dying Friederich.'

'It has been this way for many seasons now. The Purgers took the water from the river. With no one to speak for us they just took it.'

Jenna closed her eyes at this news. She wondered why they would starve this land. It was able to make food.

'Do you know why they took the water?'

'We are bonded, how would we know? '

Friederich left her.

Jenna looked out of the window towards the lands below. The fields were an ashen brown. She saw a dozen men and women tilling the soil and placing seed into the furrowed land. Going back to the bed she lay down. Jack's face sprang to mind and his last words to her; the price of a dream exacted too much. Perhaps he was right. Her forfeiture of her pre-destined role had caused much suffering to the people here. But she would never take back anything that she had done and even now she would still walk to Paris and know that everything that had been endured would be forgotten just for the sake of seeing him again.

'The only difference between the people here and Gabriel and Grandmother is that I did not love them. I would have still done the same thing. Perhaps that is the difference between a slave and a master regardless of whether each follows their destined paths or not, a slave will always capitulate and accept the fate dished to them; even if that fate is wielding the whip. Even as a master I had no heart or skill for it. No, Jack the price of love is never too high.'

She fell asleep with her whispered regrets blurring into an image of the Keep. She had just arrived at its great entrance. Its grandeur was too good to be true. Her heart had sung as she remembered the fairytales told to her of castles and the knights of antiquity. Bonded men and women stood along the ramp that led to the main hall. She looked at them. In the dream there was Friederich, Marion and Pierre and Robert.

Behind them stood the Purger who would educate her on the Charter; its figure stood like a black shadow that glistened against already defeated wills.

Sitting in the dining room surrounded by thick black beams of oak and stuffed boar heads she read a writ of punishment. It was written on pristine white parchment in fine black ink. Next to her black gloves on the table lay a whip. Marion stood before her. She was weeping and begging for mercy. She looked at the hollow eyes and cheeks of the slave. She remembered the ridges of the woman's spine as they poked out through the starved flesh as Friederich removed her smock.

Jenna Louise Tenebrae gripped the whip fiercely and bought it down so hard she felt it grab then rip the flesh of the sobbing woman before her. In her heart where the screams of disgust and guilt should lie there was stony silence.

On the bed her hands clenched the hessian cloth and her body poured with sweat as she relived the savagery. Over and over she heard the whip crack this time it was Pierre, then it was a nameless slave who had just arrived. Jenna woke sobbing; her body was shaking with the memory of her life here and what it had made her. In her desire to be kind she had not planned ahead to ensure enough food remained for winter. And then in her panic and cowardice at the thought of facing the Purgers to explain the famine she had become cruel.

She wrapped her cloak around her and in the darkness stumbled down toward the kitchen. The shame of it all clawed at her mind and heart. She saw the four figures sitting around the dying embers in the hearth. They turned and looked at her without expression.

'I cannot be forgiven for what I did to you. I have lived as a bonded now for the last twenty years of my life if that is any consolation.'

Marion got up. She limped towards her. She stopped just before her face. Jenna could see the erosive hatred in her eyes. Suddenly the sharp sting of a hand on her face struck her. She fell over. Then came the pain of an iron poker hitting her ribs. Friederich suddenly stood and grabbed Marion to stop her landing a lethal blow to Jenna's head.

'So slave does it hurt much?' Marion walked back to the hearth and sat again. She flung the poker against the flagstones, the empty metallic ring echoed up into the silent castle.

'Do you remember saying that to my sister as she lay dead? Did you even know it was my sister you beat to death that day?' sneered Marion.

'If you are no longer a Bondmaster then you should leave. You have no right to be here.' spoke Pierre.

Jenna nodded getting up sobbing.

'I remember. I remember it all. It has chased me all these years and will do so now at the end.'

'It is better to leave while it is still dark. The Purgers patrol here all the time now. They seek out strays to enslave or kill. They seek out your kind.'

Jenna looked at Friederich. He was ever loyal to her even now.

'You must hate me also Friederich?'

'Not as much as them. If it had not been for your forfeiture you would have been killed for your incompetence as a Bondmaster and we would have died also. At least this way the punishment lies on your shoulders while we simply wait to die, excused from blame. Doesn't that make us the freest of all those who live these days?'

'I am a betrayer and a liar and not worthy of any mercy.'

Jenna took the satchel of grain and water cask. She walked down the ramp into the blackness of the forest. She stopped at the ruined gateway and turned to Friederich. She was hollow inside like the dead trees around her. The viciousness of the memories that dwelt here had scarified any justification she had conjured over the years.

She took the old man's arms and looked into his face. She couldn't even cry for the pain she had caused him, so consumed with her own selfish need to be forgiven.

'You are my liberator once again Friederich. I can only offer words of gratitude and ask your forgiveness.'

'This world is depleted. You are fortunate to have anything to give or need' he replied.

9 Letter Two

I have found some bark and have been able to press it so that I can write to you. The other travellers do not ask about what I am doing. It's like we walk in cocoons with enough spun reality to keep us alive but nothing more. I think of you every day. I remember when I was walking up a cobbled street near Montmartre; the path was winding and ancient. I thought of the myriad feet that had trodden there before and how stoic those stones were to last all this time. It is unfathomable in my mind such history had passed and how irrelevant it seems now. But then I remember that history made you. Without that shaped stone and marble which was your first sight, you would not have been who you are; the carved strokes of the masterpiece as needed as much as the sunlight to make you grow. Your eyes saw every chiselled wound in that beauty and craved it more than the meagre bits of life we were allowed.

I took refuge with my sister after I was expelled from the city. She tolerated me out of family loyalty but it was only for a short while. She knew I was a forfeiter and that was an unthinkable state of being to one such as her.

You asked me once where I came from and I never told you. The truth of it is I did not want to remember who I was or where I had been. I am mostly a wilful creature who kept a wish in her heart and would not let go; but in doing so betrayed the very people that I had been entrusted to protect. I have as much blood on my hands as the Purgers. The shame I felt as Grandmother lay dying seeps like a poison in me. In her eyes I could see the mind of the sun; pure with complete mastery over her own heart. I remember my body was racked with weeping as I lit her funeral pyre knowing how utterly unworthy I had been of everything she had tried to teach me; unworthy even to spill her black ashes into the urn. That dust was more sacred to me than the earth or sun.

Is this why I glut on your love now? Do I seek the unction that will purge the venom in my soul?

The sun sets again. I will not be able to write much longer as the light grows dim.

I managed to swim to Old Africa and now make my way south. I was told once there is trade in the lands there. My mind aches as does my back and bones but my heart soars at your memory and our time together. The tenderness we shared and the kindness that we gave to each other is the essence that lingers.

Nothing will steal it away for those moments happened and have been remembered and are now written on this parchment. I copy each letter. Every word is precious, more precious than the blood they are written in. I trace my path away from you in the wounds I score on my flesh to write these words to you. The map on my arms will help guide me when it is time to return.

I don't believe them when they say that love and kindness will not help you survive.

Your voice pierces my doubt as you whispered to me once cradling me in your arms saying 'Nothing we do really matters. Our only refuge is love for we are more than beasts and less than gods. It is this which makes humans separate and lost to this world. Its grandeur is too large for our small desires and our needs too great to be satisfied just with mere survival.'

Did you know that I had heard this many times from my grandmother but never believed it? But as the utterance of your breath caressed my mind and heart I knew then this was how I was meant to be. This was how I was made and why my path lies fraught with the conflict I feel with the world. It is this that the Bondmasters see and shun. They know how its truth enflames the chains they have wrought around themselves; searing into their flesh and scarring them as a reminder of their own barbarity.

Are you a god who holds the vision of heaven and earth together as one and with a single glance can remove the veil that clouds my sight?

I am coming dear heart

She woke suddenly from another nightmare. Her body was saturated from the perspiration caused not just from the haunting memories of the Keep but also Friederich's words echoing in her mind.

Thirst drummed in her body. Jenna stilled her panting and began to listen. She got up and staggered towards the sound of gurgling in a gully that ran along the road. She stopped when she saw what was making the noise; a slave lay dying in the dried stream bed. He was bleeding from the throat. She saw that he still had a water cask at his side. She went over to him. She didn't want to look in his eyes. She pulled the cask off his sash. Suddenly a hand caught her wrist. The slave was trying to speak. She looked at him.

'You will die soon. I am sorry but I have not had water for days.'

The slave's eyes rolled back in his head as his last breathe expelled through his torn throat. She gulped down a mouthful. Her mind forced the cask away from her mouth as her body shuddered craving the rest of the water.

She stood searching the road. It was clear at the moment. Friederich's face remained from the nightmare. She had forgotten they had been lovers. It had all been dismissed when she had fled to Paris after her grandmother's death. She was no different to the Purgers; equally as callous in the destruction left behind.

She limped badly. Her leg had a malignant bruise where Marion had struck her. Her ribs flared unrelentingly from where they had broken in the storm and again from her thrashing. The day barely made it to a bright haze. The indigo lingered longer and longer. It was not until well into the afternoon that it left showing the grey green of the flax grass of the fields around her. Rising over a small hill her heart soared as the glint of metal spikes of the great wall surrounding Paris struck her vision. But the joy quickly disappeared when on another road, intersecting her route, she saw gangs of bonded and sleek black figures of their masters moving in the same direction. It was not long before she had no choice but to join them as she made her way to the city.

The Purgers that rode alongside did not look at her as she trailed behind the entourage. She saw an old couple begging at the side of the road. The old man went towards a line of slaves. The whip was so fast that it was only the man's head rolling off his neck which signaled its lethality.

She decided to go off the road and walk in the fields as she began to overtake rows of chained slaves. At the front of the procession she saw a train of bullocks pulling massive cylinders made from metal. The great beasts moved the bulwarks willingly and with grace. Jenna raced passed watching cautiously. Kat was right; they were building something to escape. The engineering in the metal structures looked out of time and place with the natural contours of the bull's muscles and empty landscape.

The memory of men in suits on the moon came to her from the books her grandmother had salvaged from the days of rebellion. The structures in the pictures were more primitive than these but their singular intent could be seen. The blade sharpness of the edges like the wings of birds shaved to precise mathematics to hold the object above the air and cut the resistance.

Suddenly the sun dipped below the horizon but instead of complete darkness the haze of indigo appeared again. It would not be long now. Suddenly the desire to yell at the Purgers and bonded to not to bother delivering their load rose in her. It was all in vain. Live what life you have left well. Taste freedom if only for a moment.

How could they not know that the black dawn was close now? She saw them begin to move further to the north. Her path lay to the south. She was glad for the change in direction. The image of what this world and herself had become lay on her like a thick plague compared to the idealized memories she had stored from the pictures of long ago. She watched the great procession of the bonded and bullocks disappear slowly into the horizon. Again the futility of human endeavour astounded her. How do you not know?

She pushed her mind again to the last time she was with Gabriel. She had relived the memory many times over the years to keep it fresh. They lay together. It was brighter back then. The yellow of the sun could be seen and felt in those days. She remembered the blue of his door was like a beacon when the sun rose fully in the sky.

'What are you doing today?'

'Resting here!' she had replied.

His smile thrilled her.

'Ok.'

He kissed her gently on the lips. She stroked his hair. She could feel the warmth of the dawn on her skin. She had felt the tickle of the curtain blowing gently in the breeze as he lay on her; his heaviness balanced and pleasant. Her body began to awake with his.

'Who are you?'

'What do you mean?'

'What is your story?'

'I was born here and I will die here.'

'Where were you born?'

'I was left on the steps of the museum. An old caretaker found me. His name was Tiberius. He was bonded and that placed me in the bonded class.'

'That is all?'

'That is all.'

'But how were you educated. How do you know what you know?'

'Tiberius.'

His nudging awoke her as he slid into her. She caught her breath slightly as he pushed and then gently stopped. She stared at his dark curly hair and olive skin. She didn't fully believe him. He must have been the class of the masters; he knew too much history.

'Is Tiberius still alive?'

'He is.'

'I would like to meet him.'

'I think he holds more secrets than we do Jenna.'

She didn't answer him but their eyes met for an instance and told each other they still had more to tell.

'Something has made you come here and stay?' as he spoke he continued kissing her. His breath tickling her as he gently nudged her again.

'I always wanted to see the sculptures and history that we read about in the tablets. But I found you instead.'

'And now you doubt my trueness?'

'I do not doubt how happy you make me.' She replied.

'Will we always love one another?'

'Yes.'

'How do you know?'

'Because my loathing for this world and myself, leaves when I am with you.'

'And what if it returns?'

'Then I would let it consume me for then I would know that you had gone forever and my life would no longer be worth living.'

'That is dramatic.' He chuckled as he kissed her neck.

'And this interrogation is unfair.'

'We will both know when it is our time to end.'

'How?'

'Did you not have that blank spot in your heart before we knew each other? When that returns then we will know.'

She felt him waiting patiently inside her, kissing her neck. How true it was, so many things had never been spoken between them and yet it didn't seem to matter. Suddenly her body wanted him; wanted the carnality to be fed. No more longings of the heart just the body. She forced her hips up and he responded.

The sound of the horses metallic galloping on the street came through the window. She looked into his eyes. There was no fear in them.

'It is not our time to die.' He whispered

'Make it so they will need to rip us apart Gabriel. Make it so we will bleed as they tear us from each other. It will be blood spilled for our love not because of their torment.'

The tears on her face from that memory came along with the searing pain of the cramps in her legs. She collapsed on the ground. She rubbed them frantically. The memory of his arms holding her and touching her flesh had never been erased by any chains she had worn as a slave or as a master.

She sat under a withered poplar tree waiting for the pain to ease. She looked across the fields and vaguely saw the outline of the city. It was not long now. She began to feel anxious. The niggling doubt came back.

'Up slave!' spoke the robotic voice. She startled. Behind her appeared three young men and two of their captors. They continued on without looking at her. She watched them disappear and then rose.

She forced herself up with thoughts only of Gabriel. Her mind traced every detail of his face, head, arms and hands. The blank spot; he had known it too. All those years it had never smudged, it had never lessened but it had completely disappeared when she had first spoken to him. And it never returned since her banishment even in her darkest moments.

She walked along the road alone now. The sight of the city was nearing. It was quieter then she expected as if it sat patiently waiting to receive her; knowing it had never let her leave.

She looked above and saw thick black clouds coalescing in the sky. She saw a bird fall from the midst of them. They were toxic whatever their source.

She turned off the road stumbling on the uneven ground. She steadied herself along the wall of the city, edging her way for at least a mile. Her foot stubbed its toe on a small corner of white marble that stuck out of the ground. It was the place she was looking for. She ran her fingers along the rough stone wall. She could not feel the notch. Panicking slightly she went slower. She felt it. She took out her knife and chiseled around the subtle gap in the wall. Sweat poured down her face as she pushed harder and harder with the blade to make the little door appear. As the clouds thickened her lungs began to burn slightly making her cough. Soon she could not see anything; even her hand on the knife. She breathed in and felt the toxic ash scorch her throat and chest. She gasped and began to cough. She dropped the knife. She began to sob.

'Not now. Not so close. Please!'

The roar shook the ground. She looked up. Fleetingly she saw the silver casing in the shape of a fan poke through the ash cloud. She realized she had just seen a flying space ship.

'But don't you see if the smoke and ash has come here then it will be everywhere. We were the last of all the planets to survive.'

She felt the knife suddenly under her hand. Grabbing it she found the notch and began to chisel the cement again. Her lungs wheezed. The blade broke through and she felt the stone give way. As she pulled it out the blood from her fingers stained the white rock. Her wheezing echoed into the empty tunnel open before her. She saw the old woman's shape at the end and her heart leapt with joy. She heaved herself forward. As she re-entered Paris the ash cloud suddenly cleared leaving the light of the indigo moon. She breathed deeply refilling her chest with air.

She looked at the old woman sitting in her decrepit pose. She would be at least one thousand years old.

'Well old woman, this old woman is ready for the ending of her journey.'

Jenna pulled on the head and the statue slid revealing a canister buried in the stone brick. She pulled it out and unscrewed the lid. Her heart almost stopped as she peered into the darkness. It was empty save for one scroll at the bottom. She took out the leather pouch that had sat next to her heart for sixty years. She opened it; the second copies of each of her letters were still intact. She took the scroll out of the canister and replaced it with the pouch.

'I have returned dear heart. You know where I will be waiting.'

She pushed the sculpture back into place. Her fingers lingered on the metal of the statue and wondered at its tenacity to remain in the world after all this time. Getting up she began to walk the streets of Paris once more. Wiping the tears from her face to clear her vision she searched for anything familiar. The ash had covered everything and the buildings had been stripped almost to the ground. Vaguely in the distance she saw the white dome of the church. She knew where to go from there. She made a path towards it. The streets were empty save for a few bonded being made to scavenge.

Suddenly a wave of sadness met her as the memory of where she had buried her grandmother came back. It was near the steps to the church. But they had gone now. The whole path had been laid to waste and all that remained was a dirty ridge of rubble. The church lay on the brink of collapse as it teetered on the edge of the excavated mound.

'Grandmother I don't know where to find you.' Her chest heaved as the sob of grief at the desecration of the old woman's grave overwhelmed her.

Be kind but don't be sentimental came to her. It will stop you giving more kindness back to the world. The last words her grandmother had ever spoken echoed in her mind as she turned to walk the final steps of her journey.

At the end of the paved street she saw the ruined gates. They had collapsed even more. All the trees had finally died; great elms and oaks that had grown to cathedral heights in defiance at the ash laden skies; casting their shade of pity on everything below their inexorable limbs. The fine silt of the toxic clouds had bitten into the white headstones. The granite statue of a young woman in repose on her gravestone was still discernible. The gentle curves of her sleeping body had not completely crumbled. It was Jenna's favourite in the old cemetery. She wanted to spend death in a perfect pose of serenity and beauty like that girl. The ruptured black obsidian of Delacroix's tomb pierced her gaze; its beauty implacable at the decay around it.

She sat upon a large flat piece of the artist's tomb and peered across the ruined city. It was still as beautiful now as it was when she had first seen it. She wondered how marvelous it must have been in the times of Delacroix and that young woman who lay sleeping on her bed of stone.

She took out the scroll, untied the string, and began to read.

10 Letter First

It is silent around me. My body bleeds but I live. I knew that I would not die at the hands of the Interrogators as it was too real, too expected. Since when does death give life a warning? If that was how the world had been made then life would flee as death gave chase and nothing would happen in the midst of the great hunt.

I will be sent to the far northern corner of the city as punishment. It is where the dirt is scoured for the minerals needed to make their fuel. It will make me sick and change me. Deep within I know that it will not kill me. Their minds are easy to read; after all, the world is dying and there are not enough left now to help them finish their machines.

I sit here on the black stone of Delacroix and wonder at such a mind. I remember Tiberius showing me pictures of his creations. My heart swelled with joy at the passion that dwelt in this man's vision and how he seduced beauty from those images of reality. You explained it so well: those humans still wondered what lay beyond the horizon.

I first saw you when I was working with the educated slaves captured to build the wall. I remember watching you arrive with the other lost souls who hemorrhaged into the city each day. I don't know what drew you to me. I think it was when I saw all the bonded around you hunch over whenever a Purger came near while you did not. I wondered at this. Your straight back and unflinching gaze reminded me of the statues on the grand old buildings who were unrelenting in their beauty and stubbornness to endure.

I followed you that day. I watched you caress every stone on the pilgrim's way to the great church that still sits on the hill. Your hand lingered gently on the beveled edges as if you wanted to take the shaped marble into you and return it to where it had been gouged from the earth. I could see in your eyes, as they beheld those sculptures, how you devoured the vision of the master architects; wanting to know their hearts and minds.

My heart soared at the defiance in your footsteps and when I saw your face I could see its plainness forged into a radiant pale light. I understood how those artists wanted to capture moments like that and sculpt the things that unleashed their love and passion.

I watched you rest on the broken steps of the church and look up at its white dome. Your lips were moving, was it a prayer, or were you talking to someone? Then I saw that you were crying. I wondered what you were sad about.

You took out a small box and you began to dig the dirt. You placed it in the ground and buried it. Then you lay on the step and wept.

Who did you weep for?

I knew then that no Bondmaster would weep over another person with such lashing sorrow and a slave would never have the privilege to know grief. I saw the precarious line you walked between those two worlds.

By now if you are reading this then you have shed more tears and trodden more difficult roads then any before it. I know that there would have been no clear path laid down for you to come back.

I know the loneliness that was born when we were torn apart would have melded to your heart with no relief. I know because it has become part of me also.

My only justification as to why I will not follow is that I will be killed as soon as I step through those ancient gates. I often walked to the edge of the city with my heart determined to discover the rest of the world only to see the flash of red blaze into life from the guard as I neared. One time I saw a man ignore it. The red eye called to the chip under his skin as he trespassed onto the fields outside. His ashes did not even remain in the air long enough for the wind to carry him across the open land.

That is why I cannot follow you now; for you must know that I would fly to you in a moment to be with you again but I would be cut down if I dared leave. My greatest fear is everything we felt, and whatever hope we cling to now will mean nothing; like the ashes of that man. I want it to be our story to tell; that we still dared to look beyond the horizon and in it we saw ourselves. We dared to sculpt our own destiny and outlive the destruction.

You asked me where I came from.

My answer to you is I do not know. I was aware of my existence like all others but at some time I began to see a double life around me. It spoke in ancient texts and moved in sculpted forms. Then I realized how bland this life was, tasteless and suffocating like dust that gets into your mouth.

I have only trodden the paths of this city but those objects of antiquity that silently watched me made me see far beyond its walls. They made me see you.

My only regret is that I have not seen what you have seen and what is to come. Your journey will be difficult but you showed me the deepest parts of your heart and the strength in your bones. You will return and I shall seek you out. Even if we are both withered like the old woman who sits and waits at our gate, it will be like no time has passed at all. I know that you will write and I will, when I am able, search for those letters and devour every single word as if it is my daily bread.

I hear them coming. It is not long now. My punishment begins as does yours. Hold dear to the sentiment in our hearts. It will never fail. It has nothing to compete for its spirit in this world. It is a blessing to know such love in a time where it is no longer considered necessary or even remembered. It lay dormant for an age but knew where to find its fulfillment when it awoke. What mighty force must lie behind such tenacity to exist? It has outlived all other ideas, wars, kings and queens and gods and masters. Even now its wisdom outlives the encoded genetic mimicry of the machines that rule our lives, and who seek refuge away from the dying sun in utter futility. They think their vision so clear but it is muddied by their arrogance. They forgot to read our story as humans in this world and how, once the sun dies so do we. Our bodies will not survive long away from the thing that birthed us.

They are shadows on a wall, no memory, no heart and no understanding of their purpose. This universe exists to create beauty and takes it away to allow more to come. I am convinced of this; nothing ends only begins again in another vision. Of all the truths that I can accept as real, it is this one I cling to most dearly. The old humans understood and like the artists relished these unique moments. They did not flee but stood and faced their destiny satisfied with their courage to withstand what the world thrust before them.

You told me of the great calm that filled the room when I spoke. How your heart stilled and the world went away. You asked me if I was a god from the stories of old.

I am no god and no hero and no villain of antiquity. I was born in a loveless world but with a heart yearning for the essence of our creation, a mind that wanted answers and eyes that looked beyond the horizon.

On the rise of the black dawn our persecutors will flee so their gaze will not be on us. Meet me at Delacroix's tomb. There we will have all the time we wish to breathe each other's scent and tell all that lies within our hearts, as it will take an age for the sun to be slowly eaten away.

Be strong Jenna. Your journey will be punishing and the hope of our reunion is as fragile as the memory of beauty in the minds of the Purgers but never forget my beloved, our time ends with the sun and not one moment before.

I am waiting dear heart

Tears fell onto the parchment as she rolled it lovingly back into a scroll. Her heart thudded hoping it would be not too much longer.

I was born in a loveless world but with a heart yearning for the essence of our creation, a mind that wanted answers and eyes that looked beyond the horizon.

And so was I Gabriel my beloved.

She watched the sun rise and saw the blackness nibble at its edges. It no longer resembled the great beaming disc that generations of humans had taken for granted. As it rose the edge of the night that lingered on the horizon would not let go. In time that line between night and day would not break and the darkness would remain.

The crunch of gravel made her look away.

He was old, withered like the statue that had guarded their secret gate into the city. His hair had gone and the punishment in the toxic pits had almost obliterated his face. His velvety olive skin was pock marked with ropes of twisted scars. In his hand he held the red leather pouch that had sat next to her heart for so long.

'Was the old woman well when you found her?'

As his voice drifted across the silence her heart stilled and it seemed the dawn did as well.

'Her back is more bent but her stubborn heart remains unbroken' she replied

The first of the black dawns washed over them like the waves of the ocean. The penetrating shadow made more magnificent, as instead of blinding their eyes, it illuminated all the colours in the rainbow that had ever existed. He took her hand just as the silken indigo of the sun's death exploded over the earth and with it Jenna felt her raiment of sorrowful longing vanish

www.ingramcontent.com/pod-product-compliance
Lightning Source LLC
Chambersburg PA
CBHW050535300426
44113CB00012B/2108